SAVED

A BIBLE STUDY GUIDE FOR CATHOLICS

SAVED

A BIBLE STUDY GUIDE FOR CATHOLICS

FR. MITCH PACWA, S.J.

**Our
Sunday
Visitor**

www.osv.com
Our Sunday Visitor Publishing Division
Our Sunday Visitor, Inc.
Huntington, Indiana 46750

Imprimi Potest
Very Reverend Brian G. Paulson, S.J.
Provincial of the Chicago-Detroit Province

Nihil Obstat
Reverend Monsignor Michael Heintz, Ph.D.
Censor Librorum

Imprimatur
✠ Kevin C. Rhoades
Bishop of Fort Wayne-South Bend
March 1, 2017

The *Nihil Obstat* and *Imprimatur* are official declarations that a book is free
from doctrinal or moral error. It is not implied that those who have granted
the *Nihil Obstat* and *Imprimatur* agree with the contents, opinions, or
statements expressed.

Our Sunday Visitor Publishing Division, Our Sunday Visitor, Inc., 200 Noll
Plaza, Huntington, IN 46750; 1-800-348-2440

ISBN: 978-1-68192-027-6 (Inventory No. T1784)
eISBN: 978-1-68192-030-6
LCCN: 2017934115

Cover design: Tyler Ottinger
Cover art: ©The Crosiers/Gene Plaisted, OSC
Interior design: Sherri L. Hoffman
Interior art: iStockPhoto.com

PRINTED IN THE UNITED STATES OF AMERICA

About the Author

FATHER MITCH PACWA, S.J., is a popular host of EWTN Catholic television network and founder and president of Ignatius Productions, a Catholic media production apostolate. His best-selling series, **A Bible Study Guide for Catholics**, includes *St. Paul*; *Growing in Faith*; *The Eucharist*; *Mary: Virgin, Mother, and Queen*; *Mercy*; and *The Holy Spirit*. He can be found online at **www.fathermitchpacwa.org**.

DEDICATION

To Father Martin Gerber, forty years a priest serving Jesus Christ and his people. *Ad multos annos.*

CONTENTS

HOW TO USE THIS STUDY
GUIDE IN A GROUP

This is an interactive study guide. It can be read with profit either alone or as part of a group Bible study. Below are suggestions for the use of this book in a group.

WHAT YOU WILL NEED FOR EVERY SESSION

- This study guide
- A Bible
- A notebook

- **Before Session 1, members of the group are encouraged to read the Introduction and Session 1 and to complete all the exercises in both.** They should bring this study guide with them to the group session.
- **Begin the session with prayer.**
- **Invite one person in the group to read one of the Scripture passages included in this session's material.**
- **Allow five minutes of silent reflection on the passage.** This allows the group's members to quiet their inner thoughts and to center themselves on the lesson to be discussed.
- **Catechesis:** Give all members a chance to share some point that they have learned about salvation. Was this something new or a new insight into something? Was there anything that raised a question? (Allow fifteen to twenty minutes for this.)
- **Discussion:** Use the discussion questions at the end of the session chapter to begin a deeper grasp of the material covered in the session. (Allow fifteen to twenty minutes for this.)

- **Conclusion:** Have all members of the group summarize the key concepts they learned about salvation in the session. Assign the next session as homework, to be completed before the next group session.

SYMBOLS USED IN THIS STUDY GUIDE

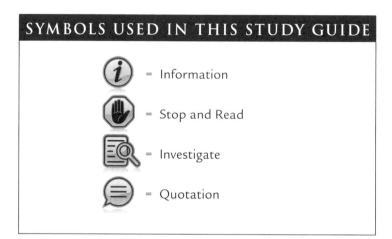

= Information

= Stop and Read

= Investigate

= Quotation

ACKNOWLEDGMENTS

Unless otherwise noted, the Scripture citations used in this work are taken from the *Catholic Edition of the Revised Standard Version of the Bible* (RSV), copyright © 1965, 1966 by the Division of Christian Education of the National Council of the Churches of Christ in the United States of America. Used by permission. All rights reserved.

Where noted, other Scripture citations are from the *Revised Standard Version of the Bible — Second Catholic Edition* (Ignatius Edition), designated as RSV-SCE. Copyright © 1965, 1966, 2006 by the National Council of the Churches of Christ in the United States of America. Used by permission. All rights reserved.

Excerpt from the introduction to the Letter to the Romans is taken from the *New American Bible, revised edition*, copyright © 2010, 1991, 1986, 1970 Confraternity of Christian Doctrine, Washington, D.C., and are used by permission of the copyright owner. All rights reserved. No part of the *New American Bible* may be reproduced in any form without permission in writing from the copyright owner.

Quotations from papal and other Vatican-generated documents available on vatican.va are copyright © Libreria Editrice Vaticana.

English translation of the *Catechism of the Catholic Church* for use in the United States of America, copyright © 1994, United States Catholic Conference, Inc. — Libreria Editrice Vaticana. English translation of the *Catechism of the Catholic Church: Modifications from the Editio Typica*, copyright © 1997, United States Catholic Conference, Inc. — Libreria Editrice Vaticana.

Excerpt from the Renewal of Baptismal Promises is taken from the English translation of *The Roman Missal*, copyright © 2010, International Commission on English in the Liturgy Corporation (ICEL). All rights reserved.

INTRODUCTION

> "For God so loved the world that he gave his only Son, that whoever believes in him should not perish but have eternal life. For God sent the Son into the world, not to condemn the world, but that the world might be saved through him."
>
> — JOHN 3:16-17

We begin this Bible study with the assumption that God wants to save the world because of his love for human beings. From his very conception and infancy, Jesus is identified as the one who saves his people. For instance, the meaning of his name in Hebrew is explained by the angel in St. Joseph's dream when he says that the still Virgin Mary "will bear a son, and you shall call his name Jesus, for he will save his people from their sins" (Mt 1:21). When the angel appears to the shepherds after the birth of Jesus, he tells the shepherds "to you is born this day in the city of David a Savior, who is Christ the Lord" (Lk 2:11).

As Jesus walked toward Jerusalem with his disciples before his passion and death, he taught them that "the Son of man came to seek and to save the lost" (Lk 19:10); "the Son of man came not to be served but to serve, and to give his life as a ransom for many" (Mt 20:28). When he entered Jerusalem on Palm Sunday, he announced that "I did not come to judge the world but to save the world" (Jn 12:47). An often-quoted verse points out Jesus' mission: "I came that they may have life, and have it abundantly" (Jn 10:10). At the Last Supper, he made it clear that his mission is not for abundant life that centers on this world but eternal life, which means knowing the Father, the only true God and Jesus Christ whom he had sent (Jn 17:3).

Salvation was not defined as a political deliverance from the Romans but as the forgiveness of sin and a new life of holiness and goodness. "Christ Jesus came into the world to save sinners" (1 Tim 1:15). St. John taught that "he is the expiation for our sins, and not for ours only but also for the sins of the whole world" (1 Jn 2:2). The extension of salvation to the whole world was a promise of the prophets: "I will give you as a light to the nations, that my salvation may reach to the end of the earth" (Is 49:6). Jesus taught this as well: "[May they] all be one; even as you, Father, are in me, and I in you, that they also may be in us, so that the world may believe that you sent me" (Jn 17:21, RSV-SCE).

Clearly, Jesus is the focal point of salvation: "I am the way, and the truth, and the life; no one comes to the Father, but by me" (Jn 14:6), and "there is one God, and there is one mediator between God and men, the man Christ Jesus" (1 Tim 2:5). Yet the vision is directed outwardly to the whole world: "For this I was born, and for this I have come into the world, to bear witness to the truth. Every one who is of the truth hears my voice" (Jn 18:37).

For that reason, this Bible study will explore a number of the rich mysteries of salvation with the sole purpose of deepening and enriching the interpersonal relationship of every human being with the tri-personal God, who is one and yet Father, Son, and Holy Spirit.

Session 1

SALVATION COMES FROM GOD AND FOR GOD

"He who created us without our help will not save us without our consent."
— St. Augustine, *Sermo* 169, 11, 13: PL 38, 923

Salvation establishes a relationship between God and sinful humans, a relationship by which God saves them from past sin, reconciles them when they continue to sin, and helps them to avoid sin in the present. His goal is abundant life and holiness, a love of truth that motivates people to share God's truth with other people, and eternal life after death. Ultimately, God, who created humanity in his image and likeness, is graciously working to transform sinners who fall short of his glory (Rom 3:23) so that they might be restored to the full image and likeness of God, who is Jesus Christ.

STUDY

Salvation Is a Relationship

In this relationship of salvation, the Lord God takes the initiative, as he has done since the time of the original sin by Adam and Eve, calling to the new sinners, "Where are you?" (Gen 3:9). In response to the sound of his approach, the no-longer-innocent couple chose to hide themselves from God, until he insisted on their coming out to meet him. True, after a thorough examination of the man, the woman, and the serpent, the Lord God imposed punishment on each of them, and yet he also showed mercy to the man and woman. He cursed the serpent with a promise about salvation for the humans: "I will put enmity between you and the woman, and between your seed and her seed; he shall bruise your head, and you shall bruise his heel" (Gen 3:15).

A WOMAN'S "SEED"

The woman's "seed" is an odd expression, since in Hebrew and other languages, the seed refers to the man's contribution to the conception of a child. This promise of a woman's seed was perplexing, until a Virgin conceived a Child by the overshadowing of the Holy Spirit millennia later, and he was named "Salvation" — that is, Jesus. The curse of the ancient serpent was at the same time the promise of a future salvation.

After the punishments, the Lord God showed mercy by clothing the couple with animal skins to cover the shame engendered by their disobedience to his commandments. Even their exclusion from the Garden of Eden was a mercy; they would not be allowed to eat the fruit of life in their sinful state until the defeat of the serpent by the Seed of the Woman at the new tree of life — the cross.

This episode shows that while God took the initiative, the couple still retained their own free will. They chose to hide, and at the Lord God's insistence, they came forth to meet him for justice and for merciful promise. The salvation of humanity entails a true relationship because both God and humans have free will within it. God chooses to freely give his grace to save sinners, and humans can either hide or come forth to meet him.

This free quality of the relationship is what makes the process of salvation seem so complicated. However, like any relationship of free persons, the complexity is the basis of the richness of the relationship. In the Introduction, we saw that the Lord God took the initiative to walk in the cool of the Garden of Eden and call out to the recently guilty man and woman, "Where are you?" (Gen 3:9).

CONSIDER

Venerable Archbishop Fulton J. Sheen wonderfully saw "Where are you?" as the most basic question of the Bible, one which distinguishes the Bible from human philosophy. Philosophy poses the human questions that seek where God or the meaning of life might be found, and looks for answers based on reason and experience. From Genesis 3:9, the Bible is a story of God asking human beings, "Where are you?" — seeking them out for a purpose greater than they can conceive.

The Lord God sought out Noah (he was the one staring at the skies for a rainstorm). The Lord sought out the pagan Abram and called him to become a blessing for all the nations of the world by worshipping the one God alone. Moses was looking for sheep when the Lord found him and spoke from the burning bush. The apostles were mending nets, or following John the Baptist, or caring for a tax collector's booth when the Lord Jesus called each of them from private business to God's mission. God takes the initiative with human beings, and asks "Where are you?" in order to draw them to himself.

STUDY

Furthermore, as with the case of Adam and Eve hiding in the bushes, he calls them while they are still sinners and does not wait until they are perfect: "While we were still weak, at the right time Christ died for the ungodly.... But God shows his love for us in that while we were yet sinners Christ died for us" (Rom 5:6, 8).

The fisherman Simon Peter recognized this reality when, after the greatest catch of his career, he knelt before Jesus and said, "Depart from me, for I am a sinful man, O Lord" (Lk 5:8). Many people are tempted to think that they must make themselves perfect, holy, and good before God will accept them. However, the biblical history points out that salvation is always offered at God's initiative to undeserving sinners. For that reason, Jesus said to some Pharisees who were offended that he sat at table fellowship with sinners: "Those who are well have no need of a physician, but those who are sick.... For I came not to call the righteous, but sinners" (Mt 9:12, 13).

Love of Israel

The Lord made clear to the people of Israel that his love for them was prior to their love for him.

 Stop here and read **Deuteronomy 7:7** and **Isaiah 63:9** in your own Bible.

Not only did the Lord declare his love for Israel before they chose to love him, but he also made it clear that they did not deserve his love; his choice of Israel was undeserved and yet filled with his gracious devotion and concern for them. He would love and guide them as a father does his small children.

The Lord declared this while the Israelites were turning away from him to worship Baal, Asherah, and the other Canaanite gods that personified the mere forces of nature, a nature he had created. Yet he continued to love Israel and guide it through a salvation history that culminated with the mission of God the Son to redeem Israel first and then the whole world.

 Stop here and read **Hosea 11:1-4** in your own Bible.

CONSIDER

The New Testament

The New Testament continues the same message that God initiates the saving relationship with people. As Jesus gave his first instruction on the Eucharist, he told the crowd of disciples, "No one can come to me unless the Father who sent me draws him; and I will raise him up at the last day" (Jn 6:44). Later, the Lord Jesus told his eleven apostles at the Last Supper, "You did not choose me, but I chose you" (Jn 15:16), which he follows with the command, "This I command you, to love one another" (Jn 15:17). St. John, one of those present at the Last Supper, wrote, "In this is love, not that we loved God but that he loved us and sent his Son to be the expiation for our sins" (1 Jn 4:10), followed by the great truth that "We love, because he first loved us" (1 Jn 4:19). Like St. John, we can only marvel at this tremendous and unearned gift: "See what love the Father has given us, that we should be called children of God; and so we are" (1 Jn 3:1).

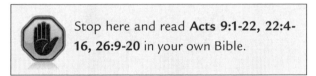

Stop here and read **Acts 9:1-22, 22:4-16, 26:9-20** in your own Bible.

Paul, an Apostle by Grace

St. Paul, whose conversion from being a persecutor of the Church and therefore of Jesus Christ himself, knew that his call to be an apostle was an act of God's undeserved grace when he wrote to the Galatians, "But when he who had set me apart before I was born, and had called me through his grace, was pleased to reveal his Son to me, in order that I might preach him among the Gentiles" (Gal 1:15).

INVESTIGATE

"UNWORTHINESS"

 Read the following passages and note where St. Paul recognizes his unworthiness to be an apostle.

PASSAGE	NOTES
1 Corinthians 15: 9	
Ephesians 3:7-8	
1 Timothy 1:12-17	

Note also how he wonders at the conversion and redemption of all Christians in Romans 8:29-32.

"LET THERE BE LIGHT"

A gaze into the amazing night sky shows the vastness of space and stirs up wonder at God, who made all of space and is infinitely more vast than the universe he created with a word, "Let there be light" (Gen 1:3), a light that exploded in a "big bang" and brought forth the orderly universe where we live. Such is the Lord God, who is "mindful" enough of man to care for each person and save all who would accept him as Creator and Savior!

INVESTIGATE

 Read the following passages and take notes on how justification and the salvation of sinners are given by God's freely offered grace.

PASSAGE	NOTES
Romans 3:24	
Romans 6:23	
Ephesians 2:4-7	
2 Thessalonians 2:16	
2 Timothy 1:8-9	

CONSIDER

Why Is Saving Grace Undeserved?

The most basic reason that God's saving grace is undeserved by people is that each individual person (and humanity as a whole) is sinful. The Old Testament saw this reality of the sinful nature of humanity, as does the New Testament.

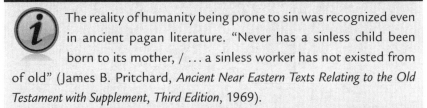

ANCIENT PAGAN TEXTS

The reality of humanity being prone to sin was recognized even in ancient pagan literature. "Never has a sinless child been born to its mother, / ... a sinless worker has not existed from of old" (James B. Pritchard, *Ancient Near Eastern Texts Relating to the Old Testament with Supplement, Third Edition*, 1969).

Akkadian prayers of different kinds express the same idea:

- "Who is there who has not sinned against his god? Who that has kept the commandment forever? All humans who exist are sinful."
- "Mankind, as many as there are, Which one of them comprehends his faults? Who has not transgressed and who has not committed sin? Which one understands the way of the god?"
- "Whoever was there so on his guard that he did not sin? Whoever was so careful that he did not incur guilt?"

(The above quotes in English and their original sources are from Robin C. Cover, "Sin, Sinners," in *The Anchor Bible Dictionary*, Vol. 6, ed. David Noel Freedman [New York: Doubleday, 1992], pp. 32-33.)

INVESTIGATE

"ONLY" HUMAN

 Look up the following passages and note what Scripture says about the nature of humanity.

PASSAGE	NOTES
Genesis 6:5	
Proverbs 20:9	
Ecclesiastes 7:20	
Isaiah 53:6	
Isaiah 64:6	

Romans 3:9	
Romans 3:22b-24	
1 John 1:8	

STUDY

The Enormity of Sin and the Infinity of the Savior

Contemporary culture has difficulty treating sin against God as a serious concern. People understand frequently enough that they are sinners, since often enough their sinful behavior gets them into a variety of serious problems: important relationships are ruptured due to various forms of infidelity; arrests and convictions are the result for those sins that society still recognizes as criminal, such as theft, perjury, or murder; and/or physical ailments and even death can result from certain sins of drunkenness, drug abuse, sexual excess, gluttony, and so on. Reality has a way of indicating to sinners that their behavior is not good for them.

Still, many modern people have a difficulty in understanding that sin is an offense against God. Some people think that God is so big that sins by puny humans cannot really affect him. Some think that humans are so small that he will not notice their sins. Others presume that he is all merciful and automatically forgives everyone, like an indulgent grandfather might do. Still others believe that since everyone is committing the same kinds of sins, particularly the sins of the flesh, God cannot condemn so many people and that he will just ignore the common sins and sinners — like a mob of gatecrashers busting into heaven. None of these ideas fit the understanding of sin that God has revealed in Scripture.

A more accurate picture flows from a common understanding of offenses: the seriousness of the offense is determined not by the person perpetrating it but by the person who is offended. For instance, fighting with my brother was wrong; hitting my parents or grandparents would have been be a far worse offense because of their greater status in the family, even though I would have been doing the very same bad action against any one of them. In civil society, a barroom brawl will land a person in the county jail for a short while; however, even threatening to strike the president of the United States will land a person in federal prison because of his status under the law.

We must apply this principle to God. Precisely because Almighty God is infinite, truly eternal, and all good, the sins we commit against him acquire an infinite and eternal quality of greater evil, not unlike the way that hitting the president acquires a federal quality to the offense and its punishment. Each person must consider his or her sins in light of the infinite God whom we offend. Humans, by their very nature, are finite, time-limited creatures incapable by nature of ever accomplishing a way to make up for an infinite, eternal sin. Furthermore, humans, even when they want to be good, still find that they have a wounded human nature that is incapable of accomplishing the good they may want to do.

CONSIDER

We can examine ourselves and realize that by nature we are incapable of ever paying the infinite and eternal debt for sin. Further, like St. Paul, people realize how difficult it is for them to do the moral good even when they truly want to avoid sin and act morally. For centuries, sinners have been able to relate very personally to St. Paul's response to the dreadful human dilemma of serving God with the mind but sinning with the flesh.

 Stop here and read **Romans 7:14-23** in your own Bible.

Two Steps to Recovery

Paul here expresses the powerlessness experienced by those recovering from addictions to alcohol, drugs, sexual and lustful urges, gambling, gluttony, or other compulsive behaviors.

The first step to recovery for addicts is the profound realization that they are powerless over the object of their addiction. Every sinner needs to arrive at the same point as Paul or the addicts: each sinner is powerless over sin, and if left to its own logic and dynamic, sin is a destructive force that will lead a person to spiritual, emotional, social, and eventually to physical death.

The second step to recovery is acknowledging that nothing within creation and no sin is more powerful than God, and that only he can free an addict from addiction and only he can free any sinful human being from sin. God's merciful grace infinitely exceeds human sin because he has sent his own infinite, divine Son to become flesh and dwell among us.

The Christian contemplates this reality, that God the Son, who is infinite due to his divine nature, truly became flesh, so that as a true human being he can represent all of humanity. Yet he did so without ever having sinned like the rest of humanity.

INVESTIGATE

JESUS' CHARACTERISTICS

 Look up the following passages about Jesus and list his characteristics.

PASSAGE	NOTES
John 1:29	
Hebrews 4:15	
Hebrews 7:26	
Hebrews 9:13-14	
1 Peter 2:22-24	
1 Peter 3:18	

1 John 3:5	
Revelation 5:6	

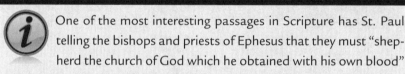

One of the most interesting passages in Scripture has St. Paul telling the bishops and priests of Ephesus that they must "shepherd the church of God which he obtained with his own blood" (Acts 20:28, author's translation). Some modern translations add "the blood of his Son," but "Son" is not in the Greek manuscripts; it is God's "own blood" (*tou haimatos tou idiou*). Clearly, this verse recognizes that Jesus Christ, the only Person of the Trinity who became incarnate and shed blood, is God and thereby has obtained the Church through his precious blood. (See Session 3, pp. 81-82, for further discussion of this text in light of the Holy Eucharist.)

Elements of the Savior

Christians understand that the mystery of salvation encompasses three essential elements of the Savior.

First, he is God the Word, infinite and without limit to save sinners, whose offenses against God possess an infinite quality due to the One who was offended by them. Unless the Savior were infinite, he would be incapable of overcoming human offenses against the Infinite One.

Second, the Savior is truly human: he became flesh (Jn 1:14). He did not merely take on a human appearance, the way the Greek myths describe their gods doing — almost always to work mischief against humans and especially against women. Jesus Christ truly became man, with a human body and soul, will and mind, without in any way ceasing to be infinite God. As a true human being he could authentically represent the human race as a go-between or mediator between human beings and God, which is what makes it possible for Jesus to be the New Adam who redeems the sins of the first Adam.

Third, Jesus, unlike the rest of humanity, is without sin and guilt, and therefore he is able to be the innocent sacrifice for others and truly atone for their sins, without the least need to atone for any sins of his own.

INVESTIGATE

JESUS' ROLE

Look up the following passages and make notes on the role of Jesus.

PASSAGE	NOTES
1 Corinthians 15:22	
1 Corinthians 15:45	
1 Timothy 2:5	

Hebrews 9:15	
Hebrews 12:24	

STUDY

Jesus as the New Adam includes two elements: (1) he removes the original sin and its punishment of death that the first Adam passed on as a heritage to all of his descendants, as well as any other sins committed by any individual person; and (2) he is the New Adam, who restores the image and likeness of God to all who accept him in faith, hope, and love as their Savior.

First, we examine the ways in which Jesus Christ, the New Adam, removes the sin of the old Adam, who introduced disobedience and original sin to the human race.

Stop here and read **Romans 5:15-21** in your own Bible.

The second element of being the New Adam is seen in Jesus' role as restoring the image and likeness of God to all of humanity who come to him and accept his offer of salvation, especially as seen in Ephesians 4.

 Stop here and read **Ephesians 4:11-16** in your own Bible.

INVESTIGATE

A COMPLETE CHANGE IN LIFESTYLE

 Not only does Jesus Christ the New Adam establish the norm of mature human living and stature, but following him also means rejecting the ways of the world.

Read the following verses and indicate how following Jesus involves a complete change in lifestyle.

PASSAGE	NOTES
Matthew 5:48	
Luke 6:36	

2 Corinthians 5:17	
2 Corinthians 7:1	
Galatians 6:15	
Ephesians 2:10	
Ephesians 4:17-19	
Ephesians 4:20-24	
Ephesians 5:1	

Philippians 3:12	
Colossians 3:9-10	
1 Peter 1:14-15	

CONSIDER

How Does Jesus Redeem Sinners?

We have already asserted the New Testament teaching that saving grace comes only through Jesus Christ because he is truly infinite God, truly human, and sinless. He is the one source and foundation of salvation, holiness, and righteousness.

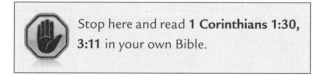

Stop here and read **1 Corinthians 1:30, 3:11** in your own Bible.

We now indicate that the way that he chose to save sinners was not easy. He accepted the fact that justice required him to take on the punishment for sin, which from the beginning was stated by God to be death, in Genesis 2:16-17: "You may freely eat of every tree of the garden; but of the tree of the knowledge of good and evil you shall not eat, for in the day that you eat of it you shall die." Eve had learned of this commandment from Adam, since she was able to relate it to the serpent at the beginning of his temptations. Since God had decreed from the outset that death was the punishment for sin, at the time when he passed judgment on Adam's sin, from that point on, God's revelation demonstrates that "the wages of sin is death" (Rom 6:23).

INVESTIGATE

MORE INFO ABOUT "THE WAGES"

To learn more about death being the punishment for sin, read the following passages. Note the number of times "death" or "die" is mentioned.

PASSAGE	NOTES
Ezekiel 18:4-20	
Ezekiel 33:7-11	
Romans 6:16-21	
Romans 8:6-13	
James 1:15	
Revelation 21:8	

Death on a Cross

From the beginning of sin by Adam and Eve until the end of time and the Last Judgment, sin will be punished by death. For that reason, it is appropriate that the Savior should take on not only sin but death by himself dying on a cross so as to fully reconcile the human race with God.

Jesus Christ was well aware that he had been born to die for the sake of sinful human beings so that they may have forgiveness and reconciliation for their sins as well as victory over death, itself the decreed punishment for sin. He knew that he came to fulfill the prophecies about the suffering, dying, and rising Messiah, and he made known to his disciples that his mission required him to die and then be raised from the dead.

 Stop here and read **Matthew 16:21, 17:22-23, 20:18-19, 20:28** in your own Bible.

STUDY

In John's Gospel, while teaching that he is the Good Shepherd, Jesus makes known the necessity of laying down his life for his sheep (Jn 10:11-18). His understanding that he must die for his sheep flows from his knowledge that he is on a mission from his Father to redeem sinful human beings. His depth of understanding his mission from the Father is especially developed on the occasion of having healed a paralytic at the Pool of Bethesda and then ordering him to sin no more (Jn 5:1-16).

In these actions, Jesus gave a clear indication of his divinity through showing lordship of the Sabbath and by an explicit assertion of his mission. While his compassion for a suffering paralyzed man led him to heal and forgive the man, his opponents saw only sin and blasphemy. In response to their being scandalized by him, he set forth more information about his relationship to his Father and his mission to redeem humanity, which we do well to hear and learn.

Stop here and read **John 5:19-24** in your own Bible.

Infinite Love

On one hand, the Son is completely dependent on the Father, and everything he does is itself a gift of the Father. On the other hand, the Father holds back nothing of his own infinity and gives all to the Son, who can receive it all only because he, too, is as infinite as the Father. The Father's total and infinite self-gift corresponds to the Son's total and infinite acceptance of all that the Father gives — such is the nature of the infinite love between them. In that context, the Son mentions the gifts that are specifically related to the salvation of human beings: the power to raise the dead and give life, and the authority to judge human hearts and souls for the final judgment based on whether a person has faith in the word of the Son and in the Father who sent him. In this way, Jesus accomplishes the Father's will.

Stop here and read **John 5:25-30** in your own Bible.

Jesus then makes it clear to his hearers that the purpose of his words is that they may be saved. In fact, the testimony of John the Baptist ("Behold, the Lamb of God, who takes away the sin of the world" [Jn 1:29, 36]) is accepted by Jesus so that people may be saved by accepting that testimony.

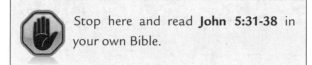

Stop here and read **John 5:31-38** in your own Bible.

Finally, the Scriptures, which at the time of Jesus' public ministry included only the Old Testament, bear witness to him through the many Messianic prophecies that foretold his birth of a Virgin in Bethlehem; his death, burial, and resurrection; and his heavenly enthronement as the Son of Man. Ultimately, the key to accepting Jesus as the Savior sent by his Father is whether a person humbly loves God or not. Humble love allows a person to accept God's Incarnate Word and Savior on God's terms without demanding that God fit our expectations.

CONSIDER

In summary, Jesus died so that all people in every place and at every epoch of time might be saved. Jesus Christ contended with sin and death and brought about a total victory by absorbing the full punishment for sin, even though he was a sinless victim who did not deserve it. Then he rose from the dead so as to defeat death, the very punishment itself. In that way, his resurrection empowers those sinners who believe in him to also have a saving hope that they will be raised from death as well.

Spreading the Message

After the Resurrection, the disciples understood the import of this message and made it the essence of their preaching wherever they went in the world. They spread the word from Jerusalem to Thessalonica, Caesarea, Corinth, Galatia, Philippi, Rome, and beyond. From these places, their message about the way God redeemed the world through his only-begotten Son, Jesus Christ, spread throughout the whole world and continues to spread. The next session will look at the ways human beings respond to this message.

THE SACRIFICE OF THE LORD

 The following passages are some of the references in Scripture to the salvific action of Christ:

- **Romans 6:10:** "The death he died he died to sin, once for all, but the life he lives he lives to God."

- **1 Corinthians 15:3-4:** "For I delivered to you as of first importance what I also received, that Christ died for our sins in accordance with the scriptures, that he was buried, that he was raised on the third day in accordance with the scriptures."

- **2 Corinthians 5:14:** "For the love of Christ controls us, because we are convinced that one has died for all; therefore all have died."

- **Hebrews 2:9:** "But we see Jesus, who for a little while was made lower than the angels, crowned with glory and honor because of the suffering of death, so that by the grace of God he might taste death for every one."

- **Hebrews 7:27:** "He has no need, like those high priests, to offer sacrifices daily, first for his own sins and then for those of the people; he did this once for all when he offered up himself."

- **Hebrews 9:25-28:** "Nor was it to offer himself repeatedly, as the high priest enters the Holy Place yearly with blood not his own; for then he would have had to suffer repeatedly since the foundation of the world. But as it is, he has appeared once for all at the end of the age to put away sin by the sacrifice of himself. And just as it is appointed for men to die once, and after that comes judgment, so Christ, having been offered once to bear the sins of many, will appear a second time, not to deal with sin but to save those who are eagerly waiting for him."

- **Hebrews 10:10:** "And by that will we have been sanctified through the offering of the body of Jesus Christ once for all."

- **Hebrews 10:14:** "For by a single offering he has perfected for all time those who are sanctified."

continued on next page

- **1 Peter 2:24:** "He himself bore our sins in his body on the tree, that we might die to sin and live to righteousness. By his wounds you have been healed."
- **1 Peter 3:18:** "For Christ also died for sins once for all, the righteous for the unrighteous, that he might bring us to God, being put to death in the flesh but made alive in the spirit."

DISCUSS

1. Why is death the punishment for sin? Do people believe that is true today?
2. Explain what "salvation is a relationship" means to you.
3. In what way is humility a key to accepting Jesus as Savior?

PRACTICE

This week select one of the Scripture passages in this session that looks at the need for the Messiah to suffer and die on our behalf, and spend some time in prayer and reflection on it. What does this passage teach you? How can you make it become more "real" in your life? What changes do you still need to make in your life to fully appreciate this great sacrifice?

Session 2

SALVATION, REPENTANCE, AND FAITH

 "The time is fulfilled, and the kingdom of God is at hand; repent, and believe in the gospel."

— MARK 1:15

Jesus made the transition from his hidden thirty years of life, mostly in Nazareth, to his three years of public preaching, teaching, and healing by being baptized by John, followed by forty days of fasting and temptation in the desert. After successfully defeating the devil's temptations, Jesus began to preach, saying, "Repent, for the kingdom of heaven is at hand" (Mt 4:17). Note that after his resurrection from the dead, Jesus concluded his message to his disciples with a similar message: "Go into all the world and preach the gospel to the whole creation. He who believes and is baptized will be saved; but he who does not believe will be condemned" (Mk 16:15-16).

Note that his words in Mark lay out the high stakes involved in the decision to believe in Jesus Christ or not — will a person be saved or condemned? Salvation offers hope of eternal life; condemnation casts a person outside of eternal fellowship with God.

 Stop here and read **Matthew 13:41, 43; 22:13-14; 25:30, 34** in your own Bible.

These are the highest stakes indeed.

STUDY

Let's examine Jesus' opening message at the beginning of this chapter in more detail, looking at its four components.

The First Component

First, Jesus announced that "the time is fulfilled, and the kingdom of God is at hand." This part of his announcement goes back to a prophecy in the Book of Daniel.

 Stop here and read **Daniel 9:24-27** in your own Bible.

Jesus was well aware that the time of his ministry and salvation fulfilled this prophecy, and therefore the time of his birth, death, and resurrection were no accident of history but the foretold window of opportunity for the redemption.

 Stop here and read **Luke 4:16-21** in your own Bible.

"SEVENTY WEEKS OF YEARS"

 "The seventy weeks of years" that are decreed for the holy city (Jerusalem) refers to a period of 490 years. Most commentators connect this prophecy with the decree by Persian King Artaxerxes I (465/4 B.C.) that gave the people of Judah permission to rebuild the walls of Jerusalem in 457 B.C. (see Ezra 7:1-28). The 490 years ends in A.D. 33, thereby linking the prophecy with the "anointed one" (Christ in Greek) who would be "cut off" in death.

Furthermore, the final Jewish Jubilee (A.D. 27) before the destruction of the Temple in Jerusalem took place — and when Jesus began to preach in Nazareth, interpreting himself as the one upon whom the Spirit of the Lord had come in order to announce a year of favor (the Jubilee) — in fact referred to the entirety of his public mission of healing, freedom, and good news for the poor.

INVESTIGATE

"THE TIME IS FULFILLED"

 Jesus' self-understanding of fulfilling these prophecies from Daniel and Isaiah are the key to teaching that "the time is fulfilled," a component of his message that was picked up and spread by his disciples. Read the following passages and take notes.

PASSAGE	NOTES
Romans 16:25-26	
Galatians 4:4-5	
Ephesians 1:9-10	
1 Timothy 2:5-6	
Titus 1:1-2	

The Second Component

The second component of Jesus' first preaching is that "the kingdom of God is at hand" or "near." The understanding of this phrase "kingdom of God" appears only once in the Old Testament, in one of the Aramaic chapters of Daniel, which predicts: "And in the days of those kings the God of heaven will set up a kingdom which shall never be destroyed, nor shall its sovereignty be left to another people. It shall break in pieces all these kingdoms and bring them to an end, and it shall stand for ever" (Dan 2:44).

The "God of heaven" will set up an indestructible kingdom that will destroy other kingdoms. These other kingdoms are described in Daniel's interpretation of a dream by the Babylonian king Nebuchadnezzar in which a statue of a man was made of various metals, symbolizing different earthly empires: Babylon was the head of gold, the Mede-Persian kingdom was the chest of silver, the Greek kingdom was the belly of bronze, and the Romans were the iron and clay legs and feet. The kingdom set up by God was a stone that turned into a mountain and destroyed the other kingdoms. This kingdom of God was in no way to be identified with any earthly kingdom or power; it was a completely different reign that would destroy all other kingdoms. Therefore, each person who accepted Daniel's message was being summoned to a new type of citizenship and a new commonwealth of God, which is in heaven.

Jesus spoke often of the kingdom of God (though sometimes he identified it as the "kingdom of heaven," both with appreciation of Jewish sensitivity to the sacredness of God's Name and in line with Daniel 2:44 where "the God of heaven" sets up the kingdom). He instructed his disciples to preach about it, and he spoke many parables about the kingdom of God. From this teaching, Jesus' followers are to learn a new identity as they live in the world as if they were no longer part of it or its kingdoms.

 Stop here and read **John 15:18; 17:16** in your own Bible.

44

The Third Component

The third component of Jesus' first preaching was his command in the plural imperative to "repent." His use of the plural indicates that it is directed to everyone rather than to one particular person. The verb in Greek — *metanoeo* — means "to turn back." This word assumes that a person is on the wrong path and, in order to get back to the right path, must turn around, retrace the false steps, and then get back to the right path.

The ancient prophets frequently gave the people of Israel a command to repent throughout their whole history. Very importantly, the Israelites did not cover up the sins of the nation or even of the national heroes; rather, they understood that everyone is a sinner, and that all, as St. Paul brought out, "fall short of the glory of God" (Rom 3:23). In Hebrew, the most typical word used for repentance from sin is translated as "turn." This is the operative term when the Israelites built the Temple as a place for sinners to "turn" from their various sins and offer sacrifice.

FULLNESS OF TIME AND *PAX ROMANA*

In addition to the more important element of fulfilling Old Testament prophecies, the secular history of Jesus' time identifies the period as the *Pax Romana* ("Roman Peace"). The previous century had been characterized by Roman conquests of the entire Mediterranean Basin, sometimes through negotiations but more often through wars against pirates, various kings, slave rebellions, and especially civil wars among the Romans themselves. Octavian (Caesar Augustus) brought an end to the Roman civil wars, whose effects had extended from Spain to Greece and Egypt, and he ruled without further conquests and nearly no wars at all. During this time of general peace, the Gospel of Jesus Christ was able to spread throughout the known world, from India to Spain and south into Egypt and Ethiopia. The *Pax Romana* was an important part of the fullness of time. It continued until the Jewish Revolt in A.D. 66, during which Jerusalem and its Temple were destroyed (A.D. 70), and the people of Israel were either killed, enslaved, or exiled.

The prophets exposed the many sins of the people and their individual kings, condemning their oppression of the poor, injustice in court, avarice, lust, and idolatry. The goal of the prophets was to evoke repentance so as to avoid various punishments, such as defeat in battle, foreign domination, and the eventual destruction of the whole nation — the ten tribes of north Israel in 722 B.C. and Judah in 587 B.C. Even after the various threatened punishments were brought down upon the people, the prophets did not gloat but offered a promise of hope for restoration and renewal.

The Fourth Component

The fourth component of Jesus' opening message is the summons to believe in the Gospel, an old English word meaning "good news." The Greek word *evangelion* meant "good news of victory," after a battle was won. The early Christians picked up this word because they believed that their message of the arrival of the kingdom of God — through Jesus Christ's preaching, life, death, and resurrection — meant the defeat of Satan's evil kingdom of darkness. Once they accepted the term *evangelion* (or "gospel") for Jesus' message and wisdom, the Christians invented a form of book now known as Gospels. These are a type of biography of Jesus, yet they do not describe his physical appearance or much about his emotional state. Rather, they focus on the central "good news" that Jesus suffered, died, was buried, and rose again from the dead.

In each of the four canonical Gospels, the passion, death, and resurrection of Jesus form the largest section of the writing. The rest of the Gospel acts as a prelude to that central event of salvation, with an emphasis on showing how Jesus fulfilled the Old Testament prophecies of the Messiah and on the ways that his healings, miracles, and teachings either raised people to believe in him or led them to fall into disbelief and hatred.

Simeon's words to the Blessed Virgin in the Temple set a major theme for Luke's Gospel, and it can be applied to the other Gospels as well:

> "Behold, this child is set for the fall and rising of many in Israel, and for a sign that is spoken against." (Lk 2:34)

People heard and saw Jesus, and they either rose to faith or fell in disbelief.

People did not merely stumble upon this decision to believe or not; throughout his public ministry until his ascension into heaven, Jesus challenged those who heard his Gospel to believe it in order to receive a miracle or even eternal life.

When messengers announced that a man's daughter had just died, Jesus ignored what they said and told the man, "Do not fear, only believe" (Mk 5:36; Lk 8:50). When another father sought help for his son, with the condition, "If you can do anything, have pity on us and help us," Jesus responded, "If you can! All things are possible to him who believes" (Mk 9:22, 23).

On other occasions, Jesus commended the faith of the people who approached him for a miracle. For instance, the Roman centurion living in Capernaum expressed confident faith that Jesus could heal his servant from a distance. As Jesus passed through Jericho, a blind man called out insistently for a healing and Jesus said to him, "Receive your sight; your faith has made you well" (Lk 18:42). After healing the man born blind, Jesus approached him and said, "Do you believe in the Son of man?" (Jn 9:35). Before raising Lazarus from the tomb, Jesus twice spoke to Martha about the necessity of faith. When she hesitated to believe that he could raise Lazarus, he again told her, "Did I not tell you that if you would believe you would see the glory of God?" (Jn 11:40).

CONSIDER

Repentant Sinners

Jesus' command to repent during his public ministry needs to be understood in light of the history of prophetic calls for Israel to turn from its sins. Jesus does not want the destruction of the sinner any more than the prophets wanted Israel destroyed, but rather he wants the sinner to turn away from evil and live a new life. Two women exemplify this in the Gospel of John.

In one case, after a Samaritan woman expresses a desire for the water that Jesus gives as "a spring of water welling up to eternal life," he tells her, "Go, call your husband, and come here." She lies to his face and says, "I have no husband." Instead of accusing her of bold-faced lying, Jesus says, "You are right in saying, 'I have no husband'; for you have had five husbands, and he whom you now have is not your husband; this you said truly" (Jn 4:14, 16, 17-18). At that point, she recognizes that Jesus is a prophet and eventually learns that he is the Christ. She then announces and preaches about him to her whole town, becoming the ideal repentant sinner who turns from her public sin to public profession of faith in Jesus Christ.

The second woman is caught in the act of adultery, and her accusers demand that Jesus condemn her to death. He turns their demand to a type of acceptance of the punishment, though with a twist: the qualification required of those executing her is that they be without sin first. One by one they leave, beginning with the oldest men there, and he, the Sinless One, is left alone with the woman. The one sinless man there tells her, "Neither do I condemn you; go, and do not sin again" (Jn 8:11).

Forgiveness of sin is not acceptance of evil but rather a summons to become good.

Lack of Repentance

On the other hand, a number of men exemplify the lack of repentance. In one episode, Jesus refuses to answer the Pharisees' question unless they first answer his question about whether John's baptism is from God or men. They refuse to answer, not because of their commitment to any position but because they fear a trap, and they will not repent.

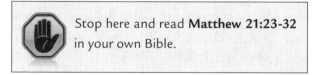

Stop here and read **Matthew 21:23-32** in your own Bible.

Love of Truth Versus Love of Self

At the heart of this dialogue is the issue of a love of truth versus love of self. The chief priests and elders argue with no concern for the truth about John's baptism for repentance from sin but for the way they will sound. Fear of the people and of loss of power or influence concerns these leaders more than does the need for repentance and the validity of John's mission. Such disregard for the truth makes their own repentance or capacity to accept Jesus' Gospel impossible. In that light, we see Jesus talk about true repentance and their need for it in connection with faith in the parable of the man, his two sons, and the vineyard.

THE FINAL DAYS

"But understand this, that in the last days there will come times of stress," St. Paul writes. "For men will be lovers of self, lovers of money, proud, arrogant, abusive, disobedient to their parents, ungrateful, unholy, inhuman, implacable, slanderers, profligates, fierce, haters of good, treacherous, reckless, swollen with conceit, lovers of pleasure rather than lovers of God, holding the form of religion but denying the power of it. Avoid such people. For among them are those who make their way into households and capture weak women, burdened with sins and swayed by various impulses, who will listen to anybody and can never arrive at a knowledge of the truth" (2 Tim 3:1-7).

This passage and others predict that the final days of human history will be times of stress brought on by the sins of the people who reject repentance and faith. Rather than using this text to determine whether one is living in the end times, one may do better to use it as an examination of conscience for anyone who has difficulty accepting the truth of the faith. Prior to trying to prove the truth of various points of the content of our faith, everyone does well to examine those personal motivations that serve to promote self-centered and immoral behaviors or tendencies. Then, if any such are discovered, repent of those sins in anticipation of examining Jesus' Gospel as to whether it is true and worthy of one's act of faith.

Christians do well to note that just as St. John taught that in addition to the final Antichrist there will be many antichrists ("As you have heard that antichrist is coming, so now many antichrists have come" [1 Jn 2:18]), so also have many times of stress occurred during which these descriptions of human sin were appropriate.

Tax collectors were so hated that a pious Jew was not allowed to marry into a family that had a tax collector; prostitutes may have been used by various men, but they were rejected by society, perhaps because they knew too many secret sins of the men. Both groups were like the first son in the parable who refused to obey, and yet when John preached repentance they received his baptism so that they could turn their lives around from sin to virtue. They accepted the truth of their sinful background and turned back to God. The chief priests and elders were so focused on their own position that they could not accept the truth of their own sinfulness and repent. Note that here, as in Jesus' opening sermon, repentance comes before faith: the ability to accept the truth of one's own life and its moral failures is the precondition for faith in the truth of Jesus' Gospel.

INVESTIGATE

BELIEVING IN JESUS' MINISTRY

 In addition to exhorting the individual to have faith, Jesus taught the necessity of believing in him throughout his ministry. Read the following passages and note which one is the most inspirational to you.

PASSAGE	NOTES
John 3:36	
John 6:27-29	
John 6:35	

John 12:36	
John 12:44	

PERSECUTION OF THE CHURCH

From its beginning and through the centuries, the Church has experienced persecution — about 75 million Christians have died for their faith in Jesus Christ. The Romans conducted ten official persecutions, the worst by far being the last, decreed by Diocletian from 303 to 313. There were the barbarian invasions from 375 to about 600; the attackers of the tenth through eleventh centuries were the Norsemen, the Magyars, and the Saracens; plus there were centuries of attacks by various Muslim invaders, such as the Seljuk Turks, the Fatimids and the Mamelukes of Egypt, Tamerlane, and the Ottoman Turks. The secularized and atheistic French Republic frequently persecuted the Church and killed many of its citizens for their Catholic faith. Thirty-five million martyrs died before 1900.

However, the twentieth century witnessed the greatest age of persecution, at the hands of National Socialism (Nazism), the nationalistic empire of Japan, and most especially at the hands of atheistic Communist governments. From the Bolshevik Revolution of 1917 through 1999, more than 40 million Christians were martyred (see John L. Allen, Jr., *The Global War on Christians* [New York: Image Books], 2013). In contrast, as bad as they were, the wars of Christianity, including the Crusades (about 650,000 killed over 250 years) and the Inquisition (fewer than 10,000 killed over its 600 years), have been responsible for 2.65 million deaths over 2,000 years of Christianity (see research at www.hawaii.edu/powerkills/welcome.html, and Steve Weidenkopf, *The Glory of the Crusades* [El Cajon, CA: Catholic Answers Press], 2014).

INVESTIGATE

 Jesus continued to deliver his message and challenge of faith even after his resurrection from the dead, since some of the disciples who saw him still had doubts. Read the following passages and note who is involved in each event.

PASSAGE	NOTES
Matthew 28:16-17	
Mark 16:9-14	
Luke 24:10-11	
Luke 24:24-26	
John 20:27-29	

The apostles and disciples accepted their mission from Jesus and traveled throughout the world, making the same appeal to repent and believe. Read the following passages and note what is particularly meaningful to you.

PASSAGE	NOTES
Acts 2:37-39	
Acts 16:31	
Acts 20:18-21	
2 Timothy 1:13	
1 John 3:23	
1 John 5:1	
1 John 5:5	

CONSIDER

Even though faith is commanded after the call to repentance, it is an absolute necessity for salvation.

 Stop here and read **John 5:24**, **Galatians 2:15-16**, and **Romans 5:1** in your own Bible.

Jesus calls us to believe, and he and his apostles teach that faith is necessary for salvation. However, one other aspect of faith needs to be mentioned in order to maintain the proper balance regarding the role of faith in living Christianity: the Bible does not teach that one is saved by faith alone, despite the claims of some denominations. True, one verse of the Bible does mention justification by faith alone, but it reads, "You see that a man is justified by works and not by faith alone" (Jas 2:24). Scripture clearly states that we are not justified by faith alone.

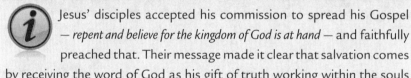

GIFT OF TRUTH

Jesus' disciples accepted his commission to spread his Gospel — *repent and believe for the kingdom of God is at hand* — and faithfully preached that. Their message made it clear that salvation comes by receiving the word of God as his gift of truth working within the souls of those who repent and believe, as shown in these sample passages:

- **1 Thessalonians 2:13:** "And we also thank God constantly for this, that when you received the word of God which you heard from us, you accepted it not as the word of men but as what it really is, the word of God, which is at work in you believers."
- **2 Timothy 3:14-15:** "But as for you, continue in what you have learned and have firmly believed, knowing from whom you learned it and how from childhood you have been acquainted with the sacred writings which are able to instruct you for salvation through faith in Christ Jesus."

STUDY

Preachers are sent to announce the word of God to stir up faith that leads to salvation. The word of God is frequently described as powerful and effective, using a variety of images:

God's Word Is a Seed That Grows and Bears Fruit
- **Mark 4:3-8, 14-23:** The parable of the sower and the seed.
- **1 Peter 1:23:** "You have been born anew, not of perishable seed but of imperishable, through the living and abiding word of God."

God's Word Is Food That Nourishes
- **Deuteronomy 8:3:** "Man does not live by bread alone, but that man lives by everything that proceeds out of the mouth of the LORD."
- **Matthew 4:4:** "[Jesus] answered, 'It is written, "Man shall not live by bread alone, but by every word that proceeds from the mouth of God." ' "

The Word of God Is Like an Effective Sword
- **Isaiah 49:2:** "He made my mouth like a sharp sword, in the shadow of his hand he hid me; he made me a polished arrow, in his quiver he hid me away."
- **Hebrews 4:12:** "For the word of God is living and active, sharper than any two-edged sword, piercing to the division of soul and spirit, of joints and marrow, and discerning the thoughts and intentions of the heart."
- **Ephesians 6:17:** "And take the helmet of salvation, and the sword of the Spirit, which is the word of God."
- **Revelation 1:16:** "In his right hand [Jesus] held seven stars, from his mouth issued a sharp two-edged sword, and his face was like the sun shining in full strength."
- **Revelation 2:12:** "And to the angel of the church in Pergamum write: 'The words of him who has the sharp two-edged sword.'"

The Word of God Is Like Water and Fire
- **Isaiah 55:10-11:** "For as the rain and the snow come down from heaven, and return not thither but water the earth, making it

bring forth and sprout, giving seed to the sower and bread to the eater, so shall my word be that goes forth from my mouth; it shall not return to me empty, but it shall accomplish that which I purpose, and prosper in the thing for which I sent it."

- **Jeremiah 23:29**: "Is not my word like fire, says the LORD, and like a hammer which breaks the rock in pieces?"

CONSIDER

St. Paul appointed his young assistant, Timothy, to be the bishop of Ephesus when St. Paul finished his three-year mission of establishing the Church there and then left for Jerusalem in the spring of the year 58. A few years later, he wrote Timothy two epistles from prison, perhaps while he was in Rome, on solidifying the Church and the preaching of the Gospel. A verse in 1 Timothy offers an important insight into our understanding of the necessity of having faith: "Great indeed, we confess, is the mystery of our religion: He was manifested in the flesh, vindicated in the Spirit, seen by angels, preached among the nations, believed on in the world, taken up in glory" (1 Tim 3:16).

In other words, the content of our faith is described as a great mystery. Why?

As described in Session 1, both revelation and our salvation itself are offered at God's initiative; these are divine gifts rather than mere human inventions. Since it is the infinite and almighty God who reveals himself as the Savior of finite human beings, his revelation in word and in history are inherently beyond the capacity of finite human minds to grasp. We certainly have the gift of reason, and we can comprehend a good deal, yet important components are perplexing and mysterious. For instance, how is the one God three infinite Persons? How is it that one infinite Person, God the Son, becomes flesh, incarnate as a finite man? How and why does he become flesh in the womb of a Virgin? How does God incarnate die on the cross? What was his resurrected body like?

These and many other mysteries are necessarily the content of faith in an infinite God as conveyed to finite human minds with finite human words.

Unfortunately, some people reduce the "mysteries" of the Christian faith to mere problems that seem too difficult for humans to understand. Far more importantly, the mysteries of the faith open up vistas of reality, human nature, the meaning of life, truth and goodness, and God himself that intrigue the mind with new depths of insight. This is not at all unlike the much smaller mysteries that explorers have sought out over the centuries and hope to examine in outer space someday, nor unlike the mysteries of physics, biology, and the other sciences that intrigue great minds with the smallest subatomic particles and the largest, most distant galaxies and stars.

The human mind loves mysteries and craves to understand them. However, unlike many of the mysteries of geography on earth or of science, the mysteries of life offer even greater vistas, and they are less resolvable: all galaxies and subatomic particles are finite; the infinite God is and will be eternally intriguing, not only during our lives on earth but also into eternal life in heaven. Because these infinite mysteries remain eternally intriguing, heaven is a place that will never become boring. New wonders will always open themselves up to the saints, who approach the mysteries of God with faith, hope, and especially with love.

INVESTIGATE

THE MYSTERIES OF GOD

 Scripture mentions the mysteries of faith in God many times. Take notes on these passages.

PASSAGE	NOTES
Daniel 2:27-28, 47	

Romans 11:25	
Romans 16:25-27	
1 Corinthians 15:51	
Ephesians 1:9-10	
Ephesians 3:1-10	
Ephesians 5:32	
Ephesians 6:18-19	

Colossians 1:24-27	
Colossians 2:1-3	
Colossians 4:2-4	
1 Timothy 3:8-9	

CONSIDER

Our task during this life is to accept and proclaim these mysteries of our faith in fidelity to God's revelation. Servants and stewards do not own their master's or employer's goods but simply administer them in full accord with his wishes. Similarly, we faithfully administer all the elements of revelation to other people in compliance with our Lord's wishes.

Another extremely important aspect of the mystery of the Christian faith finds its analogy in personal relationships. When we come to know family members, spouses, and friends deeply, we discover that each and every person is a mystery who is always beyond our capacity to know and understand completely. In fact, when people say of their loved ones, "I know exactly what he (or she) is going to say or do; it's always the same thing. I have him (or her) pegged," there may be a problem in the relationship. While some words and behaviors may be predictable, for the most part other persons are profound mysteries. The person who "knows" everything their loved ones will say or do has probably stopped listening to them, and the loved ones may be holding back their deeper thoughts because the respect for their personal dignity is gone. Far more wonderful are those older married couples, who, after fifty or sixty years together, simply shake their heads in wonder and say, "I don't know why he (or she) does what he (or she) does, but I never could have been as good as I am without him (or her)." Such couples respect and cherish the mystery of each other, which keeps them fascinated with the relationship and gives them joy.

Similarly, faith in the mysteries of God is key to the wondrous nature of the interpersonal relationship he has given the believer. The life of faith is an adventure into many unknown experiences, many of which are risky, outside one's own preferred expectations, and are sometimes even dangerous. Yet the mystery of being loved by God and of loving him in return makes the believer a more integrated, joyful, and loving person. Despite apparent losses by the world's standards or failures to live up to all the demands of the life of faith, the ever-present and infinite love of God brings a peace that "surpasses all understanding" (Phil 4:7), a peace that the world cannot give and that it cannot take away (Jn 14:27). The response is amazement and praise that we have been found by God and loved infinitely by him.

DISCUSS

1. What does "salvation" mean to you?
2. Explain the four components of Mark 1:15 in your own words.
3. How is faith both a mystery and a certainty?

PRACTICE

Refer back to the section that gives various attributes of the word of God — such as being seed, food, sword, water, and fire. Choose one of these images and find a concrete example that you can touch and hold: for example, a sunflower seed, a piece of bread, a knife (for sword), a glass of water, a candle. Reread the verse referring to the image and reflect on how God's word can become more real in your life.

Session 3

THE ROLE OF BAPTISM AND THE EUCHARIST IN SALVATION

> "The Church does not dispense the sacrament of baptism in order to acquire for herself an increase in membership but in order to consecrate a human being to God and to communicate to that person the divine gift of birth from God."
> — Hans Urs von Balthasar, *Unless You Become Like This Child*

In Session 2, we spoke of the need for faith in accepting the infinite mysteries of God, which are inherently beyond the capacity of the finite human mind to grasp. Another meaning of the Greek word *mysterion* ("mystery") is "sacrament," and that word still refers to the seven Mysteria, or sacraments, in the eastern Churches, both Catholic and Orthodox. This session will address the explicit teaching of Scripture regarding the necessity of the mysteries of the sacraments of Baptism and the Holy Eucharist for salvation.

CONSIDER

The Necessity of Baptism

Jesus Christ spoke of the necessity of baptism in a nighttime dialogue with a Pharisee named Nicodemus. First, he challenged Nicodemus with the teaching that it is necessary for a person to be born anew in order to enter the kingdom of God that Jesus had been preaching: "Truly, truly, I say to you, unless one is born anew, he cannot see the kingdom of God" (Jn 3:3). Nicodemus was unable to comprehend this requirement apart from some natural explanation of the impossibility of re-entering the womb of one's mother, so Jesus explained, "Truly, truly, I say to you, unless one is born of water and the Spirit, he cannot enter the kingdom of God" (Jn 3:5). This simple statement about the necessity of rebirth through the waters of baptism and the power of the Holy Spirit has opened up tremendous depths of the mystery of the Sacrament of Baptism, which the apostles have set before the world in Scripture and which theologians and all thoughtful Christians ponder in faith.

THE WORD OF GOD

Once, while leaving the Denver airport, a woman came up to me insisting that baptism does nothing for salvation; all one needs is faith. I asked her, "If you read in the Bible that baptism does save you, would you believe it? She answered, "No." In response, I said: "If God's truth does not matter to you, then our conversation is over." I had hoped that she would accept the truth of the following passage:

> God's patience waited in the days of Noah, during the building of the ark, in which a few, that is, eight persons, were saved through water. Baptism, which corresponds to this, now saves you, not as a removal of dirt from the body but as an appeal to God for a clear conscience, through the resurrection of Jesus Christ, who has gone into heaven and is at the right hand of God, with angels, authorities, and powers subject to him. (1 Pet 3:20-22)

STUDY

In light of St. Peter's teaching that baptism now saves us, we must ask how that is possible? What does baptism do for the person being saved?

The clearest statement of the power of baptism is found in St. Paul's Epistle to the Romans.

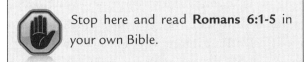

Stop here and read **Romans 6:1-5** in your own Bible.

The power of the Sacrament of Baptism flows from the death and resurrection of Jesus Christ. On one hand, the Christian enters into the power of Jesus' death on the cross and his burial by being "buried" in baptism. The waters into which one is immersed are the outward sign of dying with Christ and of being buried with him. Coming out of the water is a sign of rising from the dead in Christ Jesus. That is why St. Peter wrote that baptism is not "a removal of dirt from the body" but is "an appeal to God for a clear conscience, through the resurrection of Jesus Christ" (1 Pet 3:21). Probably within two years of writing Romans, during his imprisonment at Caesarea (the years 58 to late 59), St. Paul again explained to the Colossians that baptism is a burial with Christ so as to rise with him.

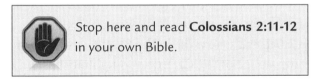

Stop here and read **Colossians 2:11-12** in your own Bible.

"Faith in the working of God" (Col 2:12), whether by the adult recipient of baptism or by the parents of an infant, is the human response that makes possible this saving bath to have its effect. This passage also uses the image of a "circumcision of Christ" that is not made by human hands but is, as St. Paul wrote in Romans 2:29, of the "real circumcision" that "is a matter of the heart, spiritual and not literal." This refers to circumcision, which was a sign of the covenant that God made with Abraham when he changed his name from Abram. Of course, the parallel between circumcision and baptism shows that baptism is now the sign of the new covenant that Jesus Christ has established. Further, the interior circumcision of one's heart — that is, the permanent character imprinted on the soul of the baptized — was a hope and exhortation from the Old Testament: "And the Lord your God will circumcise your heart and the heart of your offspring, so that you will love the Lord your God with all your heart and with all your soul, that you may live" (Deut 30:6).

In light of St. Paul's teaching that baptism is a dying and rising with Christ, the circumcision of the heart becomes the meaning of the Sacrament of Baptism. Christ works within the human hearts of the baptized and begins to transform them by the power of his saving death and resurrection. That is why St. Paul later wrote, "For we are the true circumcision, who worship God in spirit, and glory in Christ Jesus, and put no confidence in the flesh" (Phil 3:3). Similarly, Hebrews explains, "how much more shall the blood of Christ, who through the eternal Spirit offered himself without blemish to God, purify your conscience from dead works to serve the living God" (9:14). This is linked to baptism a bit later in that epistle where it says, "let us draw near with a true heart in full assurance of faith, with our hearts sprinkled clean from an evil conscience and our bodies washed with pure water" (Heb 10:22).

Clearly, the early Church understood the importance of Jesus' instruction to Nicodemus that baptism is necessary for salvation (1 Pet 3:21) and entrance into the kingdom of God. They obeyed his command to baptize everywhere they went, and this remains the teaching and practice of the Church throughout the ages ever since.

INVESTIGATE

BAPTIZE ALL NATIONS

 Jesus not only taught that baptism is necessary to be born anew, but he also explicitly commissioned his disciples to baptize all nations so that all people might enter the kingdom of God.

PASSAGE	NOTES
Matthew 28:19-20	

Mark 16:15-16	
Acts 2:38	
Acts 2:38	
Acts 19:4-5	
Acts 22:16	

STUDY

Born Anew

Jesus also taught Nicodemus that people must be "born anew." The Greek word conveys this nuance, as well as being "born again" or "born from above." As with everything necessary for salvation, the primary aspect is that God bestows his unmerited grace upon sinners. For that reason, the nuance of being "born from above" reflects the gracious component of God bringing new Christians to a rebirth through the power of Jesus Christ's death and resurrection.

The power of his death and resurrection is not merited or earned by any person: it is a free gift from heaven. As the Letter to the Hebrews makes clear, Christ ascended into heaven where he is seated at the right hand of the Father in order to offer himself as a perpetual, once-and-for-all sacrifice for sin.

From the "right hand" of the Father, inside the "Holy of Holies" in heaven itself, Jesus Christ's eternal, perpetual, and infinite self-offering is made available in every age and place for everyone who professes faith in his power to redeem sinners.

While the blood of bulls and goats was offered by Israel's high priest inside the Holy of Holies of the Temple on the Day of Atonement, Jesus is our true High Priest who offers his own blood in order to open salvation for us to "draw near" to God "with a true heart in full assurance of faith, with our hearts sprinkled clean from an evil conscience and our bodies washed with pure water" of baptism (Heb 10:22). This is how the gift of rebirth comes "from above" to save sinners.

We are also "born anew" or "born again" into the kingdom of God as "new creations" by this infinite grace. We sinners need a new start in order to prevent our past sins from defining us and our identity, so the Lord Jesus speaks of us being "born again." St. Paul wrote of this point to his disciple St. Titus, whom he had appointed to be the bishop of Crete.

 Stop here and read **Titus 3:3-5** in your own Bible.

Baptism is "the washing of regeneration and renewal in the Holy Spirit," linking "regeneration" (a noun form from the same verb for being "born anew" in John 3:3, with the addition of a prefix meaning "again" added to this noun) and the Holy Spirit in the act of renewing a person. This renewal puts the identity of our past sins in the past and the new birth and new identity in the present and future of the baptized person. Also, note that St. Paul speaks of "God our Savior" as having appeared, clearly indicating that he understood and believed that Jesus Christ is God who has appeared to save us through baptism in "water and the Spirit."

St. Paul also sees the power of baptism to transfer Christians away from their past identity as sinners into holy and righteous people.

 Stop here and read **1 Corinthians 6:9-11** in your own Bible.

The Christians of Corinth had been "washed" in baptism, which St. Paul then links with their being "sanctified" — that is, made holy by baptism, and justified. Being holy and just is their new identity that enables them to enter "the kingdom of God," and their past sins are no longer to form their identity. St. Paul also teaches that the washing of baptism "sanctifies" by making holy those people who receive it.

 Stop here and read **Ephesians 5:25-27** in your own Bible.

Paul uses the image of Christ being a loving husband to the Church who lays down his life for his bride. The purpose of dying for the Church is to "sanctify," or make her holy and cleanse her of all her faults. Christ's sanctifying baptismal washing includes the "word" that he spoke. This refers not only to the baptismal formula that he taught the disciples ("baptizing them in the name of the Father and of the Son and of the Holy Spirit") but also the whole of his doctrine ("all that I have commanded you" [Mt 28:19-20]).

New Creations

The idea of new birth through baptism, by which those who "were baptized into Christ have put on Christ" (Gal 3:27), lent itself to an Old Testament promise and hope for being formed by God into new creations. Since the Old Testament professed a strong sense that God made humans in his "image and likeness" in the first creation, it also understood that a transformation of human hearts and minds required a "new creation." Isaiah 65:17 makes this explicit: "For behold, I create new heavens and a new earth; / and the former things shall not be remembered or come into mind." The New Testament takes up this hope for transformation, as in the vision of a new Jerusalem, similar to Isaiah's, where the Lord God announces, "Behold, I make all things new" (Rev 21:5).

INVESTIGATE

HOPE FOR THE NEW CREATION

 Particularly St. Paul picks up the hope for the new creation.

PASSAGE	NOTES
Romans 7:6	
2 Corinthians 5:17	
Galatians 6:15	
Ephesians 2:10	
Ephesians 4:22-24	

CONSIDER

Water and the Holy Spirit

As can be seen in Acts of the Apostles, the early Church recognized the necessity of receiving the Holy Spirit as well as baptism. One early event occurred when persecution broke out after the martyrdom of the archdeacon St. Stephen (Acts 6-7). Another of the seven deacons, Philip, went north to Samaria and "proclaimed Christ," as well as exorcizing the demon-possessed, healing the paralyzed (Acts 8:5-8), and baptizing the people.

However, though he had the authority to baptize, as a deacon Philip did not have the power to confer the Holy Spirit; that belonged to the apostles and continues to belong to their successors, the bishops, or to the priests they delegate to confirm the baptized with the outpouring of the Holy Spirit:

> But when they believed Philip as he preached good news about the kingdom of God and the name of Jesus Christ, they were baptized, both men and women.... Now when the apostles at Jerusalem heard that Samaria had received the word of God, they sent to them Peter and John, who came down and prayed for them that they might receive the Holy Spirit; for it had not yet fallen on any of them, but they had only been baptized in the name of the Lord Jesus. (Acts 8:12, 14-16)

THE POWER OF BAPTISM

Jesus had emphasized to Nicodemus that he needed to be "born of water and the Spirit" (Jn 3:5) to show that baptism was more powerful than the many ritual baths of the Jewish people the Law required. The Holy Spirit was operative in making baptism more than a cleansing for ritual pollution due to touching corpses, childbirth, and other sexual processes of men and women, or of contact with sacred vessels and objects. Rather, in baptism, the Holy Spirit made the person into a new creation, just as the "Spirit of God" had stirred up the chaos at the old creation before the word of God was spoken to effect the existence of each creature.

Similarly, in Acts 19, St. Paul met a group of twelve men who claimed to be Christian disciples already, but he sensed that something was missing. He then engaged them in a dialogue:

> "Did you receive the Holy Spirit when you believed?" And they said, "No, we have never even heard that there is a Holy Spirit." And he said, "Into what then were you baptized?"
>
> They said, "Into John's baptism." (19:2-3)

At that point, St. Paul needed to explain to them:

> "John baptized with the baptism of repentance, telling the people to believe in the one who was to come after him, that is, Jesus." On hearing this, they were baptized in the name of the Lord Jesus. And when Paul had laid his hands upon them, the Holy Spirit came on them; and they spoke with tongues and prophesied. (19:4-6)

Whatever it was that St. Paul sensed as absent from their experience, he understood that receiving the gift and power of the Holy Spirit could only come from the baptism that Jesus had instituted and that it was a gift they very much needed. The Holy Spirit incorporates the Christian into the Church and becomes the nourishing "drink" of the Christian life. This teaching, of course, is related to the saying of Jesus when he summoned everyone to himself in the Temple and announced:

> "If any one thirst, let him come to me and drink. He who believes in me, as the scripture has said, 'Out of his heart shall flow rivers of living water.'" Now this he said about the Spirit, which those who believed in him were to receive; for as yet the Spirit had not been given, because Jesus was not yet glorified. (Jn 7:37-39)

The Holy Spirit nourishes the spiritual life of the baptized and strengthens them to live out the covenant that the Sacrament of Baptism establishes between God and the Christian. St. Paul also used an Old Testament image of the rock from which the saving water flowed for the people of Israel during their wanderings in the wilderness in Exodus and Numbers. He wrote to the Corinthians:

> I want you to know, brethren, that our fathers were all under the cloud, and all passed through the sea, and all were baptized into Moses in the cloud and in the sea, and all drank the same supernatural drink. For they drank from the supernatural Rock which followed them, and the Rock was Christ. (1 Cor 10:1-4)

Christ is the Rock from whom those who have gone through the Exodus from slavery to sin and death and passed into freedom and the promise of eternal life are able to drink deeply of the Holy Spirit.

DOES "BAPTISM" MEAN IMMERSE?

The Greek verb *baptizo* has a number of possible meanings, ranging from being a sunken ship that gets waterlogged, to dip, as when placing cloth in dye, to immerse, and to wash. In 1 Corinthians 10:2, St. Paul describes the Israelites as all having been "baptized" in the cloud and the sea. However, it is worth noting that the Israelites went through the Red Sea completely dry, while the only ones who got immersed in the water were the Egyptians. Apparently "baptism" does not always mean immerse.

CONSIDER

Seal of Baptism

Another aspect of the covenantal relationship between God and the baptized believer can be understood in the analogy from circumcision. That was a permanent sign of the covenant, at once shared by every Israelite male and yet at the same time a very personal, private, and relatively hidden sign of the covenant. In the New Testament, baptism and confirmation (as well as ordination to the ministerial priesthood) confer a sign that is more hidden than circumcision because it is placed within the immortal soul instead of on the body. It is permanent, remaining within the soul into eternity, while circumcision lasts only as long as the body. This spiritual, hidden sign is the "character" that the Holy Spirit seals inside the soul at baptism and confirmation. The word "character" is from a Greek term that refers to the impression made by a seal in soft wax, lead, clay, or other material. That impression marks the object with the name or symbol of the one who owns it. This is a way to understand that the Holy Spirit seals the soul of the believer at baptism, as St. Paul teaches: "And do not grieve the Holy Spirit of God, in whom you were sealed for the day of redemption" (Eph 4:30).

This seal of the Holy Spirit that is received in the Sacrament of Baptism is a guarantee that "our inheritance" of eternal life belongs to us, but we do not fully possess it until after death and on "the day of redemption" at the end of the world when Christ will raise all the dead to eternal life. That is why Revelation 22:14 refers to those who have "washed" their robes having the right to enter the new and heavenly Jerusalem after the general resurrection of the dead: "Blessed are those who wash their robes, that they may have the right to the tree of life and that they may enter the city by the gates."

Baptismal "washing" prepares the soul for tremendous gifts of the Holy Spirit in this life, and seals the soul into eternity, where one will inherit everlasting life with the Blessed Trinity — Father, Son, and Holy Spirit.

STUDY

The Eucharist — Requirement for Eternal Life

 Stop here and read **John 6:28-34** in your own Bible.

In John's Gospel, after multiplying loaves and fishes for a large crowd and then walking on water, Jesus went to the synagogue in

Capernaum and, in response to the questions of the people who sought him out, taught deeply about the necessity of faith and of the Eucharist for the salvation of their souls and for eternal life. The people in the synagogue asked him, "What must we do, to be doing the works of God?" to which he replied, "This is the work of God, that you believe in him whom he has sent" (Jn 6:28-29).

Faith in Jesus is absolutely essential for anyone to do that which the Lord wants from people. The people reacted to Jesus' demand for faith by requiring him to perform some sign that would guarantee their faith: "Then what sign do you do, that we may see, and believe you? What work do you perform?" (Jn 6:30). They even suggested that he give them "bread from heaven to eat" (Jn 6:31).

As always in these dialogues, Jesus takes them to ever-deeper levels of understanding. First he clarifies that Moses did not give the bread from heaven, but that his Father gives the "true bread" that gives "life to the world" (Jn 6:32-33). Once they express their desire for this bread, they ask him for it "always" (Jn 6:34), so Jesus then explains it to them.

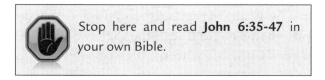

Stop here and read **John 6:35-47** in your own Bible.

When the people "murmured" at Jesus' claim to be "the bread which came down from heaven" (Jn 6:41), he insists that the Father will draw people to him (Jesus) so that he can raise them up from the dead at the end of the world: "No one can come to me unless the Father who sent me draws him; and I will raise him up at the last day" (Jn 6:44). He reiterates the necessity of having faith in order to receive eternal life — "Truly, truly, I say to you, he who believes has eternal life" (Jn 6:47). In the following verse, Jesus launches into the meaning of his teaching that he is the "bread of life."

Stop here and read **John 6:48-71** in your own Bible.

At this stage, Jesus simply asserts that he is the bread of life who is able to give eternal life to the whole world. The manna was a great gift in its day for the people who wandered in the Sinai desert, but it was not able to give eternal life to those who ate it. In fact, that first generation all died in the desert without entering the Promised Land because they had all sinned by doubting the Lord's power to overcome the Canaanites. Their faithless fear prevented them from receiving a promise for land in this life, and the manna did not give them eternal life at all: all who ate it still died. But now, Jesus is promising the people that he personifies "the bread of life" and that he will give them his flesh to eat.

HOW CAN THIS BE?

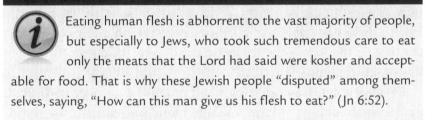 Eating human flesh is abhorrent to the vast majority of people, but especially to Jews, who took such tremendous care to eat only the meats that the Lord had said were kosher and acceptable for food. That is why these Jewish people "disputed" among themselves, saying, "How can this man give us his flesh to eat?" (Jn 6:52).

Jesus then takes them a step further by asserting that eternal life is impossible without eating his flesh and drinking his blood: "Truly, truly, I say to you, unless you eat the flesh of the Son of man and drink his blood, you have no life in you; he who eats my flesh and drinks my blood has eternal life, and I will raise him up at the last day" (Jn 6:53-54).

First, eating the flesh and drinking the blood of "the Son of Man" is the necessary condition for possessing life inside. "Life" here is not the mere biological living; the text would have read the Greek word *bios*; "life" refers to the eternal spiritual life, as signified by the Greek term *zoe* that is used here.

Second, the Lord further clarifies that eating his flesh and drinking his blood bestows "eternal life" that then makes it possible for the Son of Man to raise that person from the dead on the last day, which is the Day of Judgment at the end of the world.

Third, Jesus asserts that his flesh is "truly" food and his blood is "truly" drink, which is sometimes translated as "indeed." He really meant to make his flesh and blood available as true nourishment for eternal life, though without explaining the Eucharist at this point in his teaching.

Fourth, eating his flesh and drinking his blood offers the recipient a profound type of fellowship with Jesus, making it possible to "abide" in Jesus and for Jesus to abide in the person. This aspect of abiding, or dwelling, in Jesus and Jesus in the person is the reason we speak of "Holy Communion" with Jesus.

Fifth, Jesus clarifies that the power of the Eucharist to grant a "Holy Communion" by which humans abide in him is possible only as a gift from the Father. Jesus' relationship with his heavenly Father makes possible the gift of eternal life, in stark contrast to the manna that the Israelites ate in the desert, which was unable to bestow eternal life.

At this point, Jesus' disciples had to make a number of difficult decisions about him. "Many" of them found his teaching too "hard" and impossible to "listen to it;" these chose not to follow him any longer. Jesus then challenged the twelve apostles, and Simon Peter responded for the majority: "Lord, to whom shall we go? You have the words of eternal life; and we have believed, and have come to know, that you are the Holy One of God" (Jn 6:68-69). Finally, one of the twelve, namely Judas Iscariot, rejected him but continued to walk with him until his betrayal. Jesus was well aware of the coming betrayal and said, "Did I not choose you, the twelve, and one of you is a devil?" (Jn 6:70-71). This shows that the teaching on the Eucharist was determinative of discipleship; rejecting it meant rejection of Jesus and even betrayal of him. This makes it clear that the Eucharist is necessary for salvation.

INVESTIGATE

 Even though Jesus did not explain to the crowd that he would later institute the Eucharist, at the final Passover of his earthly ministry he did transform the meaning of the Paschal meal. Read and make notes on the following.

PASSAGE	NOTES
Matthew 26:26-28	
Mark 14:22-24	
Luke 22:19-20	
1 Corinthians 11:23-25	

CONSIDER

As St. Paul mentioned, he "delivered to" the Corinthians and to the rest of the communities he founded this mystery of the Eucharist

THE WISDOM OF THE CHURCH

 Lumen Gentium, the Dogmatic Constitution on the Church and one of the principle documents of the Second Vatican Council, sheds wisdom on these teachings (n. 7):

In that Body the life of Christ is poured into the believers who, through the sacraments, are united in a hidden and real way to Christ who suffered and was glorified. Through baptism we are formed in the likeness of Christ: "For in one Spirit we were all baptized into one body" (1 Cor 12:13). In this sacred rite a oneness with Christ's death and resurrection is both symbolized and brought about: "For we were buried with him by means of baptism into death"; and if "we have been united with him in the likeness of his death, we shall be so in the likeness of his resurrection also" (Rom 6:4-5). Really partaking of the body of the Lord in the breaking of the Eucharistic bread, we are taken up into communion with him and with one another. "Because the bread is one, we, though many, are one body, all of us who partake of the one bread" (1 Cor 10:17). In this way all of us are made members of his Body (cf. 1 Cor 12:27), "but severally members one of another" (Rom 12:4).

Lumen Gentium (n. 14) goes on to explain:

This Sacred Council wishes to turn its attention firstly to the Catholic faithful. Basing itself upon Sacred Scripture and Tradition, it teaches that the Church, now sojourning on earth as an exile, is necessary for salvation. Christ, present to us in his Body, which is the Church, is the one Mediator and the unique way of salvation. In explicit terms he himself affirmed the necessity of faith and baptism (cf. Mk 16:16; Jn 3:5) and thereby affirmed also the necessity of the Church, for through baptism as through a door men enter the Church. Whosoever, therefore, knowing that the Catholic Church was made necessary by Christ, would refuse to enter or to remain in it, could not be saved.

as a gift he had "received from the Lord." The Eucharist was not his own invention but a gift from Jesus that he needed to pass on faithfully. Similarly, the first Christians in Jerusalem included the Eucharist, known as "the breaking of the bread," in their life as a Church.

 Stop here and read **Acts 1:14; 2:41, 46-47; 20:7** in your own Bible.

STUDY

Baptism and the Eucharist are directly related to the Church. For instance, baptism incorporates a person into the mystical Body of Christ, his Church.

 Stop here and read **1 Corinthians 12:12-14, 27-28** in your own Bible.

Here St. Paul identifies the baptized as members of "the body of Christ," diverse in gift but united by the Holy Spirit to belong to the body, of which Jesus Christ is the head. In Romans 12:4-5, St. Paul also describes the one "body in Christ" with diverse members: "For as in one body we have many members, and all the members do not have the same function, so we, though many, are one body in Christ, and individually members one of another." In addition to fellowship with Jesus Christ, the Church is included in some of the passages on the Eucharist. For instance, the fellowship with Christ in his Body and Blood in the Eucharist is the reason that the Christians who receive Holy Communion are united with each other in the mystical Body of Christ, the Church.

St. Paul exhorted the bishops and priests of Ephesus to remember what is at stake in their ministry for themselves and for their flock, the Church: "Take heed to yourselves and to all the flock, in which the Holy Spirit has made you guardians, to feed the church of the Lord which he obtained with his own blood" (Acts 20:28).

God has obtained the Church with his own blood — that is, with the blood of Jesus Christ, who is God incarnate. That indicates how precious the Church is to God.

Much of St. Paul's teaching on the Church as the Body of Christ may be traced back to his own conversion, when Jesus spoke to him on the road to Damascus. While the main issue was for Jesus to convince Saul to stop persecuting him, an interesting point that Saul came to understand deeply was that Jesus radically identified himself with the Church that Saul was persecuting: what you did to the Church, you also did to Jesus. This was a variation on the theme in Jesus' teaching on the necessity of the corporal works of mercy, when he said to the righteous and to the wicked alike, "Truly, I say to you, as you did it to one of the least of these my brethren, you did it to me" (Mt 25:40, 45).

CONSIDER

Jesus' radically identifies with the leaders, preachers, and all members of the Church, and he also indicates the necessity of the Church for salvation.

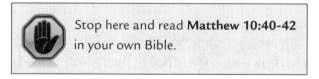

Stop here and read **Matthew 10:40-42** in your own Bible.

And, as we see in Romans 10, the preachers of the word of salvation are necessary.

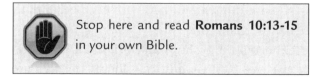

Stop here and read **Romans 10:13-15** in your own Bible.

Jesus equates receiving the preacher of the Good News with receiving him personally because he identifies with the Church members and leaders. But if the preaching of that Gospel is necessary for people to come to a saving faith, then a preaching member of the Church is necessary. Further, the preacher needs to be sent out to preach, and the Lord Jesus sends out the preachers through the Church. This was evidenced in St. Paul's life when the Church at Antioch sent him on his missions to preach in Asia Minor, and then in Europe. Though the prophets in the Church spoke the prophecy to send out Paul and Barnabas, and the members of the Church laid hands on them for this mission, this action of the Church was understood as the action of the Holy Spirit. This and other experiences helped Paul understand that the Holy Spirit, like Jesus himself, was operative in the Church. This mystery of faith helps to undergird the belief that the Church itself is necessary for salvation.

The Authenticity of the Gospel

Another aspect of the necessity of the Church in the mission to save people is its role in guaranteeing the authenticity of the Gospel that is preached. In writing to Timothy, Paul referred to "the church of the living God, the pillar and bulwark of the truth" (1 Tim 3:15). Jesus Christ did not write down his Gospel, but he entrusted it to living witnesses, the first members of his Church. Members of the Church wrote down the Scriptures, preserved them for posterity, and entrusted the verification of their authentic inspiration to them. For that reason, Paul wrote, "stand firm and hold to the traditions which you were taught by us, either by word of mouth or by letter" (2 Thess 2:15). Both the written Scriptures and the apostolic Tradition require the Church as their witness as well as their promulgators: the Church is necessary for salvation to be preached.

Having preachers of the Gospel and ministers of the sacraments of Baptism and the Eucharist requires the living members of the Church; the faith draws a person to accept baptism into the Body of Christ and to qualify to receive the Eucharist that makes its communicants united to the Person of Jesus Christ and to his Body, the Church. The Church is necessary to receive the Gospel, baptism, and the Eucharist; and the Gospel, baptism, and the Eucharist all work to effect a union with the Church. The gift of salvation flourishes into the life of the Church. This is beautifully expressed in the Book of Revelation, where the end of time is understood as the wedding feast of the Lamb, Jesus Christ. His bride is the Church, and membership in her means being clothed in righteousness — that is, in the beautiful white garment of a guest at God's great feast.

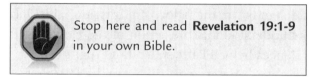

Stop here and read **Revelation 19:1-9** in your own Bible.

Not only is the Church the necessary way that Christians hear the Gospel and live the sacraments throughout this life, but the Church is also the hope for eternity. This is the community to which all those who have had faith in Christ and have loved him will dwell for all eternity in the new and heavenly Jerusalem. This is the Body of Christ on earth and in heaven, throughout time and into all eternity.

This is the Church.

DISCUSS

1. Why is baptism necessary for salvation?
2. What is the role of the Holy Spirit in baptism?
3. How is the Eucharist linked to salvation?

PRACTICE

Consider your own baptism. It is likely that your parents and/or godparents made the baptismal promises on your behalf. This week, thoughtfully consider the words of baptism and make your own, informed consent to them.

Do you renounce Satan?

And all his works?

And all his empty show?

Do you believe in God,
the Father almighty,
Creator of heaven and earth?

Do you believe in Jesus Christ, his only Son, our Lord,
who was born of the Virgin Mary,
suffered death and was buried,
rose again from the dead
and is seated at the right hand of the Father?

Do you believe in the Holy Spirit,
the holy Catholic Church,
the communion of saints,
the forgiveness of sins,
the resurrection of the body,
and life everlasting?

Session 4

THE NECESSITY OF A CHRISTIAN SPIRITUAL LIFE FOR SALVATION

"Being a Christian is not just about following commandments: it is about letting Christ take possession of our lives and transform them."

— POPE FRANCIS, tweet (April 10, 2013)

Before his ascension, the risen Lord Jesus told a large crowd of disciples, "I am with you always, to the close of the age" (Mt 28:20). This refers not only to his presence in the Holy Eucharist but also to a spiritual presence that disciples enter through a lively prayer life. Certainly, this understanding of God's abiding presence with people is deeply rooted in the Old Testament, where certain individuals and the whole of Israel are promised that God will be with them.

Stop here and read **Exodus 3:12, 1 Kings 8:57-58, Isaiah 41:8-10**, and **Haggai 1:13** in your own Bible.

In the Gospels, Jesus Christ becomes the focus of God's presence among his people. In St. Matthew's Gospel, the angel explains to St. Joseph that Mary is bearing the Messiah in fulfillment of the prophecy in Isaiah, saying: " 'Behold, a virgin shall conceive and bear a son, / and his name shall be called Emmanuel' (which means, God with us)" (Mt 1:23).

In showing that the virginal conception of the child was accomplished by the power of the Holy Spirit, the angel also explains that the child is "Emmanuel," and the meaning of this name — "God with us" — highlights the fact that the child is God's presence among the people. In fulfillment of the angel's command — "You shall call his name Jesus, for he will save his people from their sins" (Mt 1:21; Mary had been given the same name by the angel Gabriel in Lk 1:31) — the Son, who is the presence of God, has a name indicating that God is present in Jesus to save people. His names indicate that his presence is linked to salvation.

STUDY

"Where Two or Three Are Gathered"

On his final journey to Jerusalem, Jesus also told his disciples, "Again I say to you, if two of you agree on earth about anything they ask, it will be done for them by my Father in heaven. For where two or three are gathered in my name, there am I in the midst of them" (Mt 18:19-20).

Jesus taught his disciples to ask God to care for their needs, trusting that he will care for them as does a loving Father. However, he expands his teaching on prayer with two elements. First, he makes it a condition of prayer that the disciples "agree on earth" about the gift they seek from the Father. This implies that they must enter into a dialogue among themselves and consider their requests carefully through a type of discernment of the Father's will for them. Second, Jesus promises to be present in the midst of his disciples who have "gathered in my name." The implication is that his presence will help them in the discernment process about the true good that they ought to seek from the Father and that his presence will assure disciples of a hearing from his Father. Prayers of petition call for a prayerful attentiveness to Jesus' ongoing presence within the community of disciples that he calls his Church.

St. John tells of another teaching about Jesus' ongoing presence with his disciples, which is described after Jesus enters Jerusalem on Palm Sunday: "If any one serves me, he must follow me; and where I am, there shall my servant be also; if any one serves me, the Father will honor him" (Jn 12:26). Serving the Lord requires a disciple to follow Jesus, a teaching he gave many times earlier in public ministry. One aspect of following Jesus means to keep his commandments. Keeping his words and commandments sets one up for a fellowship that makes a disciple "at home" with God.

 Stop here and read **John 14:23** in your own Bible.

John 12:26 also speaks of Jesus' presence with the disciples: "Where I am, there shall my servant be also." The disciple is meant to abide in Jesus' presence in an ongoing relationship by which he or she not only receives Jesus' love, but the Father's as well. The ultimate goal of Christian fellowship with the presence of Jesus Christ is a full engagement with the life of the Blessed Trinity.

 Stop here and read **John 17:20-24** in your own Bible.

The presence of Jesus became all the more poignant in the minds and experience of the disciples when the risen Lord Jesus Christ appeared to them on the day of his resurrection.

 Stop here and read **John 20:19-22** in your own Bible.

Eight days later, his disciples were again in the house, and Thomas was with them. The doors were shut, but Jesus came and stood among them, and said, "Peace be with you" (Jn 20:19, 21).

These and other apparitions of the Lord to many disciples proved to them that not even his death on the cross was able to prevent his presence among them. The tomb could not contain him, and the doors that the disciples had locked shut could not keep him away from them, nor could a journey away from Jerusalem isolate disciples from his presence. The presence of Jesus could not even be prevented by Saul's rejection of Christ and persecution of the Church: Jesus became present to him on the road to Damascus and changed his whole life. Jesus also came to him at other times, such as during his mission in Corinth.

Stop here and read **Acts 18:9-10** in your own Bible.

INVESTIGATE

THE PRESENCE OF GOD

Not only is the presence of God part of every Christian's experience in prayer and in special experiences — such as the appearances of Jesus to St. Paul — but it also sets the tone for one's hope in heaven. Take notes on what encourages you from the following readings.

PASSAGE	NOTES
Luke 23:43	

John 14:3	
2 Corinthians 5:6-8	
Philippians 1:21	
1 Thessalonians 4:17	
Revelation 14:13	
Revelation 21:3	

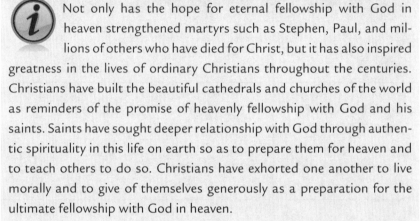

Not only has the hope for eternal fellowship with God in heaven strengthened martyrs such as Stephen, Paul, and millions of others who have died for Christ, but it has also inspired greatness in the lives of ordinary Christians throughout the centuries. Christians have built the beautiful cathedrals and churches of the world as reminders of the promise of heavenly fellowship with God and his saints. Saints have sought deeper relationship with God through authentic spirituality in this life on earth so as to prepare them for heaven and to teach others to do so. Christians have exhorted one another to live morally and to give of themselves generously as a preparation for the ultimate fellowship with God in heaven.

Scholars, monks, nuns, and so many others have devoted their lives to serve Christ with their "whole hearts, minds, and souls" in order to be found worthy of heaven. This is why St. Paul prayed "that Christ may dwell in your hearts through faith; that you, being rooted and grounded in love ..." (Eph 3:17). This is why he could teach the Church: "Indeed I count everything as loss because of the surpassing worth of knowing Christ Jesus my Lord. For his sake I have suffered the loss of all things, and count them as refuse, in order that I may gain Christ" (Phil 3:8).

CONSIDER

The Way of the Cross as a Way of Life

Another essential component of a Christian spiritual life was taught by Jesus in the context of his announcements that he had to suffer, die on the cross, and rise again.

Stop here and read **Luke 9:22-26** in your own Bible.

This passage shows that Jesus is the "pioneer" and "perfecter" of our salvation and faith, since he first states that he will suffer his passion and die on the cross before he rises from the dead into glory; only then will his disciples be required to take up their crosses and follow him.

STUDY

Beginning the Journey

The Christian who has repented of sins, come to faith in Jesus Christ, accepted the truth of the Gospel, received renewal through baptism, and entered into communion with Jesus through the Eucharist has simply begun the journey. That whole process is the "turning around" from the evil path that leads to destruction and eternal death so that one can begin the journey toward eternal life. This journey is not mere "tourism through life" but is a pilgrimage of faith. Tourists visit interesting places, take photos and "selfies," tell their friends of their trip, and return to their formal normalcy. Pilgrims, on the other hand, have a goal in mind, some sanctuary or shrine — such as Lourdes, Fátima, Guadalupe, the Holy Sepulcher, and others — where they hope to renew their faith and devotion.

For pilgrims, the journey itself is part of the process of letting the experience improve their lives. They pray more intensely, do penance, and contemplate the meaning of their pilgrimage goal so as to let that goal transform them. The Second Vatican Council named Chapter VII of *Lumen Gentium* "The Pilgrim Church" (nn. 48-51) to show that "Already the final age of the world is with us (cf. 1 Cor 10:11) and the renovation of the world is irrevocably decreed" and "the Church already on this earth is signed with a sanctity which is real though imperfect." However, until the Lord manifests the "new heavens and a new earth in which justice dwells (cf. 2 Pet 3:13)," the pilgrim Church still "has the appearance of this world which is passing and she herself dwells among creatures who groan and travail in pain until now and await the revelation of the sons of God (cf. Rom 8:19-22)" (*Lumen Gentium*, n. 48).

Truly the holiness of Christ is already present in the Church, yet the imperfections of the sinners who have been converted still affect every member until perfection is attained in heaven with God and his saints.

Take Up Your Cross

Knowing the effects of sin on human beings, our Lord Jesus Christ understood the import of teaching his disciples in Luke 9:23-24:

> "If any man would come after me, let him deny himself and take up his cross daily and follow me. For whoever would save his life will lose it; and whoever loses his life for my sake, he will save it."

Even after one's first conversion through repentance and faith, the effects of sin remain in a person, and the cure that Jesus proposes is to deny oneself and take up the cross daily.

Self-gratification is not the same as self-love. Self-gratification accedes to immediate desires that, due to the concupiscence (which means disordered desires) that remains after original sin, induce us to crave the good things of this world either too little or too much, but not in accord with our true good. People crave cauliflower and broccoli too little but ice cream and cake too much. People want sex too much but respect, responsibility, and commitment too little.

Jesus Christ therefore instructs his disciples to deny themselves, which is experienced as the carrying of a cross.

Any addict will tell of the mighty struggle to overcome addiction and at a popular level might say, "This is killing me!" That expression gets to Jesus' point, but not as a protest to make the pain stop. Rather, he instructs disciples to embrace the pain of self-denial that is killing one's ego, or as the New Testament frequently describes it, "the flesh." Though many people think of "sins of the flesh" as belonging only to the sexual realm, in reality "flesh" refers to everything that corrupts a person and causes moral decay the way animal flesh decays and rots once the soul is gone from the animal or human. (Of course, the animal soul ceases to exist at death.)

Sins of the Flesh

St. Paul describes the flesh with a variety of physical, emotional, and even intellectual sins. Read the following and make notes of the sins that are mentioned.

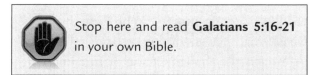

Stop here and read **Galatians 5:16-21** in your own Bible.

Some of the sins of the flesh are sexual and altering one's consciousness through alcohol or drugs; other sins of the flesh include false worship of idols or the attempts to use "sorcery," magic potions, or astrology and such; other sins of the flesh are interior and emotional, such as anger, jealousy, and causing enmity with others; while some are purely intellectual, such as dissension or "party spirit" (Greek *haireseis*, or "heresies"). The result of living in accord with the flesh is one's inability to "inherit the kingdom of God" (Gal 5:21). Though St. Paul never mentions condemnation in hell, the reader must draw his or her own conclusions about the fate of those who do not inherit the kingdom of God. He again points out the consequences of the contrast between living "according to the Spirit" versus "living according to the flesh" in Romans.

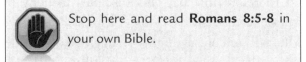
Stop here and read **Romans 8:5-8** in your own Bible.

In this context, the Christian who seeks salvation must realize that he or she is not merely accepting one moment of Christ's forgiveness of sins but is rather embarking on a holy pilgrimage that leads one to eternal life in heaven. Not only is the goal a holy one, but the journey is one of becoming ever more holy. This pilgrimage through life in this world requires the converted person to die to oneself daily and deny gratifying the disordered desires of the flesh. The disordered goals that are presented by our egos, the culture, or even by the evil spirit are unworthy of human life and dignity. Great fame on earth fades quickly after death.

Ask yourself how many Roman emperors, Holy Roman emperors, kings of England, or U.S. presidents you can name. These once-famous people are mostly forgotten. Who were the wealthiest people in each of the last twenty centuries? Who were the greatest baseball, football, or basketball players of the 1940s?

At one time, people thought it was worth knowing the names of these people; some were even considered heroes. Today they are mostly forgotten, and their achievements by the world's standards no longer matter to the world. In this light, consider Jesus' teaching as he makes clear what is at stake in a Christian's decision to take up the cross daily:

> "For what does it profit a man if he gains the whole world and loses or forfeits himself? For whoever is ashamed of me and of my words, of him will the Son of man be ashamed when he comes in his glory and the glory of the Father and of the holy angels." (Lk 9:25-26)

While the world forgets its own stars and leaders, God will never forget his own, no matter how little they might be in the world or the Church. He will remember his own into all eternity in his everlasting glory. Just as Christ's resurrection made his passion and death worth all the pain, so will the Lord's glorification of his saints in heaven make everyone's dying to self worthwhile.

Christians do not simply deny their ego: the purpose is for Christ to live inside each person, enabling everyone to live a new kind of life guided by faith in Jesus, the Son of God. Of course, since Jesus loves and gives himself to each person who accepts him, the spiritual life will be characterized by ever-increasing love and self-giving, which his interior presence will empower.

CONSIDER
Replacing Vice with Virtue

 Stop here and read **Galatians 5:22-25** in your own Bible.

A further explanation of "crucifying the flesh" means that its passions and desires must die so that the new choices of holy virtues may replace the passions. Recall that immediately before this verse, St. Paul had listed the fruits of the Holy Spirit — "love, joy, peace, patience, kindness, goodness, faithfulness, gentleness, self-control" (Gal 5:22-23) — each of which constitutes "living by the Spirit" and "walking by the Spirit," free of conceit and envy. The vice of pride or conceit is the primary vice to crucify; after that, the other vices are less likely to be defended, and the virtues are more likely to be accepted.

We can consider St. Paul's background and see that he was an up-and-coming leader among the Pharisee party in Jerusalem due to his intelligence and intense zeal. However, once Christ confronted him on the road to Damascus and he accepted conversion, he came to see the absolute truth of Jesus' parable: the kingdom of God is the treasure found in a field or the pearl of great price for which it was worth selling everything. Dying to himself meant that everything he possessed, especially all of the prospects of success, were a loss and "refuse" or "trash" compared to knowing Christ. The lifelong process of coming to know Jesus and of letting him transform our vices into virtues is a minimum of the spiritual life.

STUDY

The cost of God's redemption of us sinners is paid by God himself: Jesus Christ, the Son of God made flesh, paid the price for our salvation by dying on the cross for us. Is there a cost for us? Of course, each of us must die to self and enter the mysteries of God's saving actions through faith in him. Is it worth the cost? God thinks that we are of such value that it was worthwhile for his Son to die on the cross for us. He also tells us in the above-mentioned passages that he thinks we will find our faith and dying to self well worthwhile, not only in eternal life but also in this life. Consider the anxiety, fear, and aimlessness of so many contemporary people. In contrast, Christians who die to themselves experience more peace than is feasible for those who appear to possess "everything," and yet miss out on inner peace. St. Paul writes on this topic, too.

 Stop here and read **Romans 5:1-2** in your own Bible.

Of course, this peace does not exempt Christians from suffering. One of the tragic mysteries of life is that very frequently, Christians are singled out for suffering, torture, and death precisely because they live out their faith well and are at peace. Yet, as seen throughout the history of the Church, the persecuted and the martyrs are able to find a joy that eludes their persecutors or the people who seem to have "everything."

 Stop here and read **Romans 5:3-5** in your own Bible.

St. Paul — who was beaten with rods, scourged, stoned, ship-wrecked, and imprisoned many times before his martyrdom under Emperor Nero — could "rejoice" in sufferings because it developed his character. He understood that he had character defects and that he needed to grow and improve. Therefore, out of his suffering he learned endurance, which developed his character and produced hope in him. Yet even these positive developments occurred not because of Paul's own personal strengths but because God had "poured" his love into the apostle's heart through the Holy Spirit. In other words, he understood that the positive growth that took place even through his sufferings was a gift of God and not a mere human power. In light of that, Paul then explained that redemption is itself an undeserved gift of God through Jesus Christ.

 Stop here and read **Romans 5:6-8** in your own Bible.

The demonstration that proves God's love is the death of Jesus while we were still sinners. Christ does not demand that sinners become perfect before they are loved: they are loved while they are still in their sin. What he does demand is that they repent of their sin. They come to accept that the sin is wrong and that they are responsible for having committed it, and that they are sorry for their sin.

Confession of Sin

Jesus Christ spoke of the necessity of humble and thoroughly honest confession of sin in Luke 18 in a parable directed to those "who trusted in themselves that they were righteous and despised others" (v. 9).

 Stop here and read **Luke 18:10-14** in your own Bible.

We do well to place ourselves within this parable by first picturing ourselves as the Pharisee, to think back on those times when we justified ourselves and looked down upon the rest of the sinners. For instance, those who watch programs like *The Jerry Springer Show* or read gossip magazines sometimes admit that it makes them feel good about themselves: they know they are sinning, but at least they are not as bad as the people on the stage. That would be a modern and more secular version of the Pharisee's attitude. Then let us imagine ourselves as the publican, who knows how unworthy he is to find God's mercy, and yet comes to God with full and honest admission of sin and trust in God. Then imagine oneself in that attitude, but instead of praying in the Temple, picture Calvary, standing before Jesus Christ crucified, confessing one's sins before him. Realize that his suffering is offered up to make atonement for the precise sins to which one has just admitted and confessed, and that he continues to love sinners infinitely and unconditionally — which is the only way that God knows how to love. This is one aspect of understanding the nature of God who "is love" (1 Jn 4:8, 16).

 Stop here and read **Romans 5:9-11** in your own Bible.

The forgiveness we receive by Jesus shedding his blood on the cross is the basis of hope for being saved from the wrath of God that our sins deserve. Even though our sins have caused pain and chaos in our own lives and in the lives of other people, and even though God has a juridical right to condemn us on the basis of justice by itself, we are saved from his wrathful punishment because the self-gift of Christ by dying on the cross for us is stronger than our sins. The reconciliation with God is profound, and our salvation is his free and undeserved gift. Allowing this reality to deepen within our hearts and minds is a source of our peace through Christ and is a wellspring of joy that surpasses our understanding.

CONSIDER

St. Paul further develops the implications for the spiritual life that flow from the redemption that Christ has won for us in Romans 6:6-8:39, which is worth considering as a source for our own spiritual lives. We will examine sections of this deep and life-giving passage as a way to begin understanding it, in the hope of opening it up for a deeper meditation on self-understanding in light of Christ's demand to die to oneself.

 Stop here and read **Romans 6:6-10** in your own Bible.

This section begins with St. Paul pointing out that "our old self" needed to be "crucified" with Christ for a twofold goal: the sinful aspect of the body must be destroyed and enslavement to sin must be avoided. Dying to sin makes it possible to live with Christ, and that occurs only if we unite our decision to die to sin with the infinite power of Jesus' death on the cross. How do we unite dying to sin to the cross of Christ? Through faith that his death has the power to forgive our sins and to enable us to die to the desire to commit future sin. The second aspect, freedom from enslavement to sin, was a livelier image for St. Paul's contemporaries than it is for most modern people, since about one-third of the people living in the Roman Empire were slaves. Some slaves were simple laborers, and others were highly educated intellectuals forced to tutor the children of the wealthy. As all addicts and the people who have developed habits of sin know, their repeated sins and addictions form habits that enslave them. They find it very difficult to cease their gluttony, gambling, pornography use, gossip, lying, and other such habitual sins. Only when they realize that they are powerless to overcome the sin and turn to God to change them can they make authentic change. Like Paul, they experience this as a crucifixion of their old self, thus rejecting the sin.

Stop here and read **Romans 6:11-23** in your own Bible.

This passage develops the idea of becoming "dead to sin and alive to God in Christ Jesus" with the realization that sin will no longer "reign," or rule, over one's body (Rom 6:11, 12). When sin rules, then passions are let loose, and we let our emotions guide decisions instead of thinking clearly about God's true purpose for the body and the world so that God's commandments direct our decisions. When the members of the body are at the control of the passions, then these various members become instruments or even "weapons" of wickedness. Each of us can consider how the various members of the body can be used either for righteousness or for wickedness: the hands that caress a loved one can also strike or kill someone; the mouth that gently encourages can also gossip; the eyes that radiate love can also send out daggers of hate. The choice of dying to oneself in Christ places the body under the power of grace so that the person can act righteously; the choice to be a slave of sin submits the members of the body to wicked behavior. Which will a person choose?

Stop here and read **Romans 7:7-12** in your own Bible.

After a discussion of the relationship of the Old Testament Law and the need to turn to Christ, who brings a new covenant and new relationship with God, St. Paul discusses his own difficulty with the Law, or Torah. The Law commanded him not to covet, but it was the commandment that evoked covetousness in him, since the power of sin that was inside of him used the commandment as an occasion to entice him to covet.

At the point of clarifying that the Law remains good and spiritual, he describes an experience of many (if not most) people regarding sin.

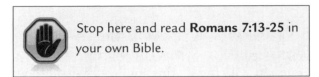

Stop here and read **Romans 7:13-25** in your own Bible.

There are certainly many people who do not desire to do that which is good as God defines the good or as defined by the legitimate rights, desires, and needs of other people. By seeking only that which they believe is good for themselves, most other people are tempted to see their actions as purposefully bad or even wicked. These are not the people of whom St. Paul writes here.

In Romans 7:13-25, St. Paul speaks of himself and for many other people who truly want to be good as God defines moral right and virtue. Such people see and accept that the Law of God is spiritual and good. However, they find themselves incapable of obeying the Law, no matter how sincerely they desire its good and right action. In fact, he even discovers that he does the evil he hates instead of the good he desires because he is "carnal, sold under sin," and his body makes him "captive to the law of sin" that dwells inside his flesh (Rom 7:14, 23). At a simple level, apply this analysis to keeping to a diet — yet alone to areas of sin, bad habits, or addictions.

At this point, St. Paul cries out as if in despair of ever becoming a good and virtuous person: "Wretched man that I am!" His question, "Who will deliver me?" flows from the same sense of weakness, but quickly turns away from any temptation to despair toward God through our Lord Jesus Christ (Rom 7:24). His redemption of sinners is the escape from human helplessness to do what is good and right.

STUDY

St. Paul develops his understanding of Christ's power to save us from our moral weakness in Romans 8.

Stop here and read **Romans 8:1-4** in your own Bible.

First, St. Paul states in this passage that those who are "in Christ Jesus" by their repentance of past sin and their faith need not fear any condemnation. Of course, this implies that those who are not related to Christ through faith ought to fear condemnation. Christ pours out his Spirit upon morally weak human beings to set them free from the "law of sin and death" in their "flesh" that prevents them from doing the good and right things of God's Law. The weak flesh cannot be good; God the Holy Spirit enables sinners to truly change their lives.

Stop here and read **Romans 8:5-13** in your own Bible.

Second, in Romans 8:5-13, we read that the human mind receives a gift of being reoriented from pursuing the desires of the flesh to seeking the things of the Spirit. This, too, is not a mere human capability but is a gift and grace from the Holy Spirit, who enables the mind to seek peace "which passes all understanding" (Phil 4:7) and eternal life. The alternative is to continue pursuing the flesh, which necessarily makes a person hostile to God in this life and in life after death.

Stop here and read **Romans 8:14-17** in your own Bible.

Third, the saving relationship of faith in Jesus Christ and his gift of the Holy Spirit effect a change of relationship with God and a new identity. God is more than the Creator or Judge: the Holy Spirit works within the depths of a person and identifies God as "Abba," the familiar Aramaic word for "Father" that is well-translated as "Daddy." Israeli children still address their fathers with this tender word to this day. The Holy Spirit's inner working, by which humans can understand themselves in this loving, intimate relationship with God as "Abba," thereby gives each person a new identity as children of God. Some philosophies try to teach that every human is a child of God by nature, but the reality of sin that St. Paul described in Romans 6-7 indicates rather that every human being is born a rebel against God. God is the one who transforms sinners into his children by the power of his own Spirit operating inside the depths of their hearts.

ADOPTION INTO GOD'S FAMILY

What the Holy Spirit effects within the Christian is an adoption into God's family, as St. Paul also wrote in Galatians 4:4-6.

A corollary to being God's adopted children is that we are thereby "heirs" and "fellow heirs with Christ" (Rom 8:17). We will therefore inherit eternal life in the kingdom of God our Father and live a glorified form of being made in the "image and likeness of God." All Christians who accept this new identity are royalty, princes, and princesses in our Abba's heavenly kingdom. However, to reach that true goal of life, St. Paul insists that "we suffer with him in order that we may also be glorified with him" (Rom 8:17). We come right back to the necessity of dying to oneself, picking up the cross daily and following Jesus. This is not something extra that the saints have to do; this is warp and woof of the regular Christian life. The good news is that no Christian accomplishes it on his or her own power alone; the Holy Spirit is truly operating inside the human heart to make it possible.

Stop here and read **Romans 8:18-25** in your own Bible.

The process of dying to oneself points to the prospect of pain due to fighting against one's vices (which people often cherish), or failing to gratify one's desires, or from the rejection and even hatred or persecution that a commitment to Jesus Christ often evokes. However, St. Paul offers a basis for a hope by which we are saved: living through the sufferings of the present life leads directly to a glory that God will bestow upon the children of God. This glory that is in store for the redeemed will even improve the rest of creation, just as human failure and sin brings harm and disharmony to creation. Until that full gift of glory is granted, the whole of creation is "groaning in travail" (Rom 8:22), a phrase describing the process of childbirth. The ultimate rebirth and new creation will be the full manifestation of "adoption" by God, which is the redemption of human bodies in the resurrection from the dead. The resurrection of Jesus Christ anchors the hope of resurrection for every one of the redeemed and keeps the Church moving ever closer to Christ and salvation. In this way, hope saves us, as does faith.

ANCHOR — SYMBOL OF HOPE

The image of an anchor as a symbol of hope is found in Hebrews 6:19-20: "We have this as a sure and steadfast anchor of the soul, a hope that enters into the inner shrine behind the curtain, where Jesus has gone as a forerunner on our behalf, having become a high priest for ever after the order of Melchizedek."

Jesus Christ is risen from the dead and has ascended into heaven to the "right hand of the Father" in the Holy of Holies of heaven. Therefore, since he is already there, our hope in him is compared to a rope that anchors us in heaven. In fact, this image goes back to a practice of ancient Israel: when the high priest entered the Holy of Holies of the Temple in Jerusalem, a rope was tied around his ankle, so that if he died while inside the Holy of Holies, the priests outside could drag his body out without entering a place they were forbidden to enter under pain of their own death. In reference to Christ the High Priest, the rope ties us to him as our hope that he will hoist us into heaven rather than have us drag him down out of heaven.

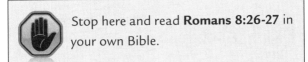

Stop here and read **Romans 8:26-27** in your own Bible.

These verses recognize that the spiritual life depends not on human techniques but on the gift of God: "We do not know how to pray as we ought." The "weakness" St. Paul mentions comes from the moral disorder in the "flesh." The inability to pray as we "ought" implies that a certain quality of praying is expected by God. Prayer is the term that describes the way human beings communicate with God, both by speaking to him and by listening. However, the flesh so weakens the will that it no longer wants to even engage in deep communication with God, and it so clouds the capacity to pay attention to him that people need God the Holy Spirit to intercede "with sighs too deep for words" and to do so "according to the will of God."

Most people know that their words frequently fail to express all that they feel or think, especially when speaking to someone they love. If anything, the more deeply the love is felt, the less are words able to express the feeling. How much more is this true of the relationship with God: the deeper is one's love of God, the less able are words to express that love. Yet God desires from each person a depth of prayer that only God the Holy Spirit can bestow. God the Holy Spirit can search the human mind and will more truly than even the person can know himself or herself, and the Spirit can stir within the person to seek out the actual will of God for the sake of the highest good instead of the immediate but false goods desired by the flesh. St. Paul's recognition of the flesh's influence on human "weakness" even regarding something as spiritual as prayer indicates that the need to die to oneself applies to the spiritual life and prayer as much as it applies to the moral spheres of life. However, by engaging in the process of dying to oneself, Christ comes to life in the depths of the human spirit, and an interior transformation occurs.

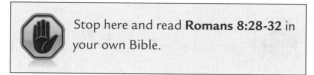

Stop here and read **Romans 8:28-32** in your own Bible.

In this passage, Paul expresses the confidence that every Christian needs as a foundation for the hope that saves: "In everything God works for the good with those who love him." If God could redeem the world through the death of his own Son, whom "he did not spare," then we can gain a new understanding of everything that happens in life, including the disappointments, pain, and suffering. Nothing is outside of God's providence to use for the good of his adopted sons and daughters, whom he has chosen "to be conformed to the image of his Son." Jesus Christ always remains the model of transformation that God is effecting within each Christian. For that reason, he calls, justifies, and glorifies everyone who turns to him in faith. Therefore, even when life is very difficult (as it frequently was for Paul), we can trust that God is working in the difficulties and not merely despite them. He is transforming us into being images and likenesses of his Son, and he sets before each person a tremendous hope.

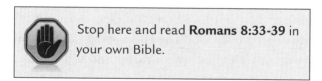

Stop here and read **Romans 8:33-39** in your own Bible.

The basis for trust and hope is further developed in this conclusion of Romans 8 with a series of rhetorical questions: "Who shall bring any charge against God's elect? ... Who is to condemn? ... Who shall separate us from the love of Christ?" The expected answer to each of them is "No one!" God has justified us; Christ has died, risen, and ascended to prevent the condemnation of us sinners; and nothing can separate us from the love of God in Christ Jesus.

DISCUSS

1. What is one action you can begin today to improve your spiritual life and union with God, based on what you learned in this chapter?
2. How does one "take up one's cross"? What does this mean in your own life?
3. If you truly believe that you have been adopted into God's own family, how does this change the way you view God? Your fellow Christians?

PRACTICE

Much of this chapter focuses on Paul's Letter to the Romans. The introduction to the Letter to the Romans (New American Bible, revised edition) says this:

> Of all the letters of Paul, that to the Christians at Rome has long held pride of place. It is the longest and most systematic unfolding of the apostle's thought, expounding the gospel of God's righteousness that saves all who believe (Rom 1:16-17); it reflects a universal outlook, with special implications for Israel's relation to the church (Rom 9-11).... Paul's Letter to the Romans is a powerful exposition of the doctrine of the supremacy of Christ and of faith in Christ as the source of salvation. It is an implicit plea to the Christians at Rome, and to all Christians, to hold fast to that faith.

Because of the importance of this letter in Christian theology, make a commitment to read it in its entirety after finishing this Bible study.

Session 5

GOOD WORKS AND ETERNAL LIFE

> "When we attend to the needs of those in want, we give them what is theirs, not ours. More than performing works of mercy, we are paying a debt of justice."
>
> — St. Gregory the Great, *Regula Pastoralis* (3, 21)

An unnecessary controversy was created in the Reformation by adding the word "only" and "alone" to certain biblical truths with the saying, "Justification comes by faith alone by grace alone." Truly, every Catholic should hold that justification comes by faith in Jesus Christ and that faith, like hope and love, is a theological virtue granted to people by God's undeserved grace. However, as mentioned in Section 2, the words "justified by faith alone" are found together in the Bible

MARTIN LUTHER AND "FAITH ALONE"

Quite famously, Martin Luther taught that "justification by faith alone by grace alone" was the principle upon which his gospel rose or fell. For that reason, he rejected not only seven books from the Old Testament but, what is less well known, for a few years he rejected seven from the New Testament as well: James, Hebrews, 2 Peter, 2 John, 3 John, Jude, and Revelation. He later restored them to his New Testament, but his introduction to the Letter of James called it "a letter of straw." He believed that his idea of the Gospel message ought to determine the canon of Scripture. The Catholic perspective is that the contents of the canon must determine the contents of our faith and Gospel.

only once: "You see that a man is justified by works and not by faith alone" (Jas 2:24). The important point is not so much the refutation of "justification by faith alone by grace alone" but rather the need for every Christian to understand the ramifications of the full scriptural teaching about the justification that opens the way to heaven.

CONSIDER

An important element of living the Christian life is the "obedience of faith," which was taught in both Vatican I and II. The following is from Vatican I (*Dei Filius* [Dogmatic Constitution on the Catholic Faith], Chap. 3, "On Faith"):

> 7.   And so faith in itself … is a gift of God, and its operation is a work belonging to the order of salvation, in that a person yields true obedience to God himself when he accepts and collaborates with his grace which he could have rejected.

> 8.   Wherefore, by divine and Catholic faith all those things are to be believed which are contained in the word of God as found in Scripture and tradition, and which are proposed by the Church as matters to be believed as divinely revealed, whether by her solemn judgment or in her ordinary and universal magisterium.

> 9.   Since, then, without faith it is impossible to please God (Heb 11:6) and reach the fellowship of his sons and daughters, it follows that no one can ever achieve justification without it, neither can anyone attain eternal life unless he or she perseveres in it to the end.

This is from Vatican II, *Dei Verbum* (Dogmatic Constitution on Divine Revelation):

> To make this act of faith, the grace of God and the interior help of the Holy Spirit must precede and assist, moving the heart

and turning it to God, opening the eyes of the mind and giving "joy and ease to everyone in assenting to the truth and believing it." (n. 5)

For that reason, every person of faith needs to accept and proclaim "the whole counsel of God" (Acts 20:27), which includes the acceptance of God's gift of saving faith as well as the "obedience of faith" by which each person lives out the way of salvation as the Church and Scripture teach.

Again, Vatican II, in *Dei Verbum*, explains the role of the Church in interpreting the Scripture and the apostolic Tradition:

> But the task of authentically interpreting the word of God, whether written or handed on, has been entrusted exclusively to the living teaching office of the Church, whose authority is exercised in the name of Jesus Christ. This teaching office is not above the word of God, but serves it, teaching only what has been handed on, listening to it devoutly, guarding it scrupulously and explaining it faithfully in accord with a divine commission and with the help of the Holy Spirit, it draws from this one deposit of faith everything which it presents for belief as divinely revealed. (n. 10)

Popes and councils cannot alter the word of God: Sacred Scripture is not some plaything that they can mold in any manner they wish. Rather, the Church "serves" the word of God, not by the intelligence or character of the people who hold office in the Church but by the gift of the Holy Spirit. Vatican II clearly states that the reason the Church serves the revealed word of God in Scripture and sacred Tradition that comes from the apostles is due to the nature of the word as a revealed gift from God:

> Therefore, since everything asserted by the inspired authors or sacred writers must be held to be asserted by the Holy Spirit, it follows that the books of Scripture must be acknowledged as teaching solidly, faithfully and without error that truth which

God wanted put into sacred writings for the sake of salvation. (*Dei Verbum*, n. 11)

Note the last phrase, where it states that the reason to believe and serve Sacred Scripture is that its purpose is to help people reach salvation. The same point was made at Vatican I (Dogmatic Constitution on the Catholic Faith, Chap. 3, "On Faith"):

6. Now, although the assent of faith is by no means a blind movement of the mind, yet no one can accept the gospel preaching in the way that is necessary for achieving salvation without the inspiration and illumination of the Holy Spirit, who gives to all facility in accepting and believing the truth [citing the Second Council of Orange, Canon 7].

Therefore, Vatican II asserted:

The Church has always venerated the divine Scriptures just as she venerates the body of the Lord, since, especially in the sacred liturgy, she unceasingly receives and offers to the faithful the bread of life from the table both of God's word and of Christ's body. She has always maintained them, and continues to do so, together with sacred tradition, as the supreme rule of faith, since, as inspired by God and committed once and for all to writing, they impart the word of God himself without change, and make the voice of the Holy Spirit resound in the words of the prophets and apostles. Therefore, like the Christian religion itself, all the preaching of the Church must be nourished and regulated by Sacred Scripture. For in the sacred books, the Father who is in heaven meets his children with great love and speaks with them; and the force and power in the word of God is so great that it stands as the support and energy of the Church, the strength of faith for her sons, the food of the soul, the pure and everlasting source of spiritual life. (*Dei Verbum*, n. 21)

The Catholic Church also rejects the doctrine of "Scripture alone" (*sola Scriptura*) that has been proposed by some Christians since the fourteenth century. They have added the word "alone" to the requirement to believe that the Bible is the inspired word of God. William of Occam, a Franciscan friar, was the main proponent of this doctrine, apparently inspired by Muslim philosophers who held to the Quran as the sole revelation of God. However, the Bible itself never teaches that one believes in the Bible alone. If that is the case, then this idea of *sola Scriptura* is a concept introduced from outside the Bible, and as such, it contradicts its own principle of accepting the Bible alone. Rather, we read this in Sacred Scripture: "So then, brethren, stand firm and hold to the traditions which you were taught by us, either by word of mouth or by letter" (2 Thess 2:15).

STUDY

Practical Faith

James 2:24 talks about the necessity of good works along with our faith in justification. However, that is only one verse among many in James that we can examine. The Epistle of James is a book of Christian wisdom that, like Old Testament wisdom books (Proverbs, Sirach, Book of Wisdom, Job, and Ecclesiastes), offers help to people of faith in living out some of the practical aspects of life in the light of faith. This is not the wisdom based solely on the world's assumptions but has God as its starting point.

God's wisdom is found throughout the Gospels in Christ's teachings, as well as in the writings of his apostles, but especially in St. James' epistle of wisdom.

 Stop here and read **James 1:21-25** in your own Bible.

This passage picks up themes that relate to the preceding discussion on the role of the word of God in our lives. Obviously, St. James expresses strong revulsion at the wickedness of sin when he calls it "filthiness." Greco-Roman culture, not at all unlike modern society, accepted widespread sinful, violent, lewd, gluttonous, and vulgar behavior with open-minded, nonjudgmental ease. Whether it was the gladiatorial "games" of death, the lavish feasts of the wealthy, or orgies and illicit affairs, people were very accepting and broad-minded — unless the behavior directly affected one's honor. In the latter case, an offended husband or disrespected citizen might seek revenge for the bad behavior (women generally did not have the same rights as men in such cases); but otherwise, immorality was acceptable and gossip was shared with a click of the tongue.

Christians, such as St. James, saw sinful behavior in the light of Christ as filthy wickedness that must be avoided. One antidote to the filthy wickedness of the world and the flesh was the word of

WISDOM AND THE WORLD'S CLEVERNESS

In 1 Corinthians 1:22-25, St. Paul instructs us that the wisdom that comes from God is ultimately more intelligent than that of the world, no matter how strongly the world insists on its own cleverness. For instance, consider that the wars, genocide, and oppression of the twentieth century were based primarily on philosophical ideologies. Nationalism, which raised the nation to a higher value than God or his Church, was a strong ideology in the two world wars in which 70 million people died. National Socialism (Nazism) and Communism both rejected God and became responsible for 235 million deaths between 1917 and 1991 (see Session 2, p. 51, for the number of deaths during religious wars).

God "is the source of your life in Christ Jesus, whom God made our wisdom, our righteousness and sanctification and redemption" (1 Cor 1:30), and on that basis Christians have improved their own lives, their life in society, and their cultures. Following St. Paul, we truly seek to live wisely, but not with worldly wisdom.

God that was implanted in Christian hearts to point out the contrast between righteousness and wickedness so as to save the souls of believers from the pollution of sin. The word of God helped people know goodness and virtue, and it exhorted them to live holy lives.

The word of God is not merely a beautiful idea but is a way of life to be lived. Therefore, it is insufficient only to hear the word and give verbal assent to it. St. James points out that Christians must *do* the word of God. He identifies God's word as "the perfect law, the law of liberty" that guides its doers to the freedom for holiness. At best, the society of his day (like many parts of modernity) offered mere license to sin rather than freedom for virtue. Committing sin does not release tension or anxiety, even though some people make that claim as an excuse for their wrong behavior. Rather, sin builds up a bad habit that becomes difficult to change, and that enslaves the person to wickedness. The freely chosen decision to be morally good helps build a habit of virtue that makes it ever easier to act righteously with freedom.

The Truth of God's Word

The importance of doing the truth of God's word appears elsewhere in the New Testament as well. Jesus ended the Sermon on the Mount with insistence that his disciples obey his words: "Not every one who says to me, 'Lord, Lord,' shall enter the kingdom of heaven, but he who does the will of my Father who is in heaven' " (Mt 7:21). He goes on to say:

> "Every one then who hears these words of mine and does them will be like a wise man who built his house upon the rock; and the rain fell, and the floods came, and the winds blew and beat upon that house, but it did not fall, because it had been founded on the rock. And every one who hears these words of mine and does not do them will be like a foolish man who built his house upon the sand; and the rain fell, and the floods came, and the winds blew and beat against that house, and it fell; and great was the fall of it." (Mt 7:24-27)

CONSIDER

On two other occasions, Jesus' mother became involved. Once, when she wanted to see him, he said, "For whoever does the will of my Father in heaven is my brother, and sister, and mother" (Mt 12:50; see also Mk 3:35; Lk 8:21).

On the other occasion, a woman in the crowd raised her voice and said to him, " 'Blessed is the womb that bore you, and the breasts that you sucked!' But he said, 'Blessed rather are those who hear the word of God and keep it!' " (Lk 11:27-28).

In both cases, the mention of Jesus' mother evoked his summons to do the will of his Father, which is the authentic imitation of Mary, of whom Elizabeth was inspired to proclaim, "And blessed is she who believed that there would be a fulfilment of what was spoken to her from the Lord" (Lk 1:45). At the Last Supper, he told the apostles, "If you know these things, blessed are you if you do them" (Jn 13:17). Upon hearing that, one apostle went out into the night to betray him; the other eleven abandoned him in Gethsemane, and one even denied him. Only later, when Jesus came to them after his resurrection, did they learn to know and do the things Jesus said, or, in the case of Judas, killed himself in despair.

St. Paul agreed with this truth fully when he connected it to being justified and righteous before God: "For it is not the hearers of the law who are righteous before God, but the doers of the law who will be justified" (Rom 2:13). In another situation, he warned Christians against acting for the sake of appearance, "not in the way of eye-service, as men-pleasers, but as servants of Christ, doing the will of God from the heart" (Eph 6:6). Doing "the will of God from the heart" therefore means, "Whatever you do, in word or deed, do everything in the name of the Lord Jesus, giving thanks to God the Father through him" (Col 3:17). Later, St. John confirmed this: "Beloved, do not imitate evil but imitate good. He who does good is of God; he who does evil has not seen God" (3 Jn 1:11).

STUDY

Faith and Good Works

St. James presents his teaching on the necessity of good works with faith in light of experience and the Old Testament. As is typical of wisdom literature, the discussion begins with rhetorical questions about the ability of faith to profit or save a person who does not have good works. "What does it profit, my brethren, if a man says he has faith but has not works? Can his faith save him?" (Jas 2:14). The second rhetorical question takes up a hypothetical situation that brings up true need for good deeds: "If a brother or sister is ill-clad and in lack of daily food, and one of you says to them, 'Go in peace, be warmed and filled,' without giving them the things needed for the body, what does it profit?" (Jas 2:15-16).

From these hypothetical situations, he concludes: "So faith by itself, if it has no works, is dead" (Jas 2:17). He backs up his conclusion by pointing out the weakness of faith alone:

> But some one will say, "You have faith and I have works." Show me your faith apart from your works, and I by my works will show you my faith. You believe that God is one; you do well. Even the demons believe — and shudder. (Jas 2:18-19)

An example of having the correct statement of faith in the oneness of God can be held even by the demons because it is true, but holding a true act of faith is not sufficient to save anyone. Even if the demons hold what is true, they still will not be saved. James moves along with another rhetorical question, which he addresses to a "shallow man" who still holds that faith without works is acceptable, and answers it with examples from the Old Testament.

 Stop here and read **James 2:20-26** in your own Bible.

Abraham was justified by obeying God's word when he was tested by the extreme request to offer his son Isaac as a sacrifice; Rahab the prostitute of Jericho was justified not only by her faith that the Lord had saved Israel in its previous struggles but also by her help to the two Israelite spies whose lives she spared. Most importantly, in the middle of the examples, James makes clear the key principle of this section: "A man is justified by works and not by faith alone" (Jas 2:24). That principle is developed by his rhetorical question and answer in James 3:13: "Who is wise and understanding among you? By his good life let him show his works in the meekness of wisdom." A good life is displayed in good works as the fulfillment of the "royal law" from God: "If you really fulfil the royal law, according to the scripture, 'You shall love your neighbor as yourself,' you do well" (Jas 2:8).

The conclusion for Christians of each generation is to believe the full truth about God, to enter a relationship of faith with God through Jesus Christ by the power of the Holy Spirit, and to do good works. Not only are good works necessary for a Christian to live faith authentically, but the doing of good works is necessary for salvation, and the commission of evil works will exclude a person from entering the kingdom of God. We will examine those passages where the need for good works and the prohibition of evil works determines one's salvation.

STUDY

Sermon on the Mount

The Sermon on the Mount sets out many of Christ's basic moral and spiritual teachings and principles.

 Stop here and read **Matthew 5:1-12** in your own Bible.

The introduction begins with the proclamation of a series of beatitudes, by which Jesus announces a reversal of the world's expectations — the poor and meek are losers, justice will never triumph, mercy is for weaklings, and purity is absurd — by the power of God's reality: the poor and meek will inherit the earth, the merciful will find mercy, the hunger and thirst for righteousness will be satisfied, the pure of heart will see God, and even persecution for the sake of Christ or for righteousness will be rewarded by God. Next, Jesus addresses his disciples with new identities.

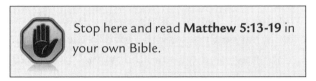
Stop here and read **Matthew 5:13-19** in your own Bible.

In the first part of this passage, the disciples, like salt, are to help preserve the world from its corruption; like light, they are to bring light into the darkness of the world. It is important to note that Jesus wants them to be concerned for the world, whether by preserving it from corruption or by giving it light. On the other hand, the next verses (Mt 5:17-19) also insist that the disciples maintain their concern for entering the kingdom of God as well as care for this world. Jesus makes it clear that his commission to preserve and enlighten the world requires of his disciples their adherence to God's moral law.

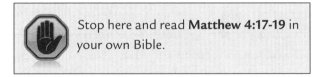
Stop here and read **Matthew 4:17-19** in your own Bible.

In the fourth chapter of Matthew's Gospel, Jesus' initial message, "Repent, for the kingdom of heaven is at hand," assumes repentance from sins that contravened God's holy Law (as St. Paul explained in Romans 7; see Session 4, p. 103). In Matthew 5, Jesus teaches that God's Law is good, a teaching that he maintains later on when he answers the first question of the rich young man: "Teacher, what good deed must I do, to have eternal life?" (Mt 19:16). Jesus answers the question completely in line with Matthew 5:17-19:

> "If you would enter life, keep the commandments." He said to him, "Which?" And Jesus said, "You shall not kill, You shall not commit adultery, You shall not steal, You shall not bear false witness, Honor your father and mother, and, You shall love your neighbor as yourself." (Mt 19:17-19)

Of course, when the young man said to him, "All these I have observed; what do I still lack?" Jesus said to him: "If you would be perfect, go, sell what you possess and give to the poor, and you will have treasure in heaven; and come, follow me" (Mt 19:20-21). Jesus typically takes people beyond the bare minimum to a perfection that reshapes them into the image and likeness of God in ways that only Jesus can exemplify. That is why he wants his disciples, including this young man, to "come, follow me." This young man did not accept Jesus' invitation, and his name is unknown; Peter, Andrew, James, John, and others who followed him are still well known.

Demand for Perfection

Back in the early section of the Sermon on the Mount, we see Jesus make a similar demand for perfection among his disciples: "For I tell you, unless your righteousness exceeds that of the scribes and Pharisees, you will never enter the kingdom of heaven" (Mt 5:20). The Pharisees were lay people who sought to live the Law of Moses seriously and strictly at a time when the priests (the Sadducees) were very worldly, while the scribes were the scholars within the Pharisee movement. Most Jews accepted the Pharisees as the best examples of living the Law. However, Jesus tells his disciples that their righteousness must exceed that of the scribes and Pharisees: that is, like the rich young man whom Jesus called to perfection, the disciples must live to a standard that Jesus himself sets.

Jesus then explains the moral righteousness that he expects in Matthew 5:21-48.

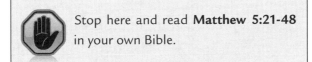

Stop here and read **Matthew 5:21-48** in your own Bible.

Each section of this passage begins with a statement of one of God's commandments, after which Jesus explains that the righteousness of his disciples must go more deeply: Beyond "You shall not kill" is his demand to reject anger, revenge, and name-calling; beyond, "You shall not commit adultery" is his prohibition against lust, which would make possible the purity that allows the blessed to see God; beyond granting a writ of divorce to protect a woman's honor, Jesus prohibits divorce; beyond forbidding false oaths, Jesus demands that his disciples always tell the truth without any need for any oaths; beyond merely limiting the level of revenge that is permitted, Jesus prohibits all revenge and demands that his disciples treat their enemies with love and concern. He concludes his teaching on moral righteousness with this summary: "You, therefore, must be perfect, as your heavenly Father is perfect" (Mt 5:48). This is the ultimate meaning of being re-formed into the image and likeness of God, whose perfection is the norm and ideal for the human beings who "repent and believe" and accept the call to follow his Son, Jesus Christ.

Righteousness

Next, Jesus explains the kind of righteousness that exceeds that of the "scribes and Pharisees" that belongs to the realm of the disciples' spiritual lives: "Beware of practicing your piety before men in order to be seen by them; for then you will have no reward from your Father who is in heaven" (Mt 6:1). The word translated as "piety" here is the same Greek word that was translated as "righteousness" in Matthew 5:20. A more literal translation would be: "Beware not to do your righteousness before men." It is also worth noting that St. Paul definitely teaches that "a man is not justified by works of the law but through faith in Jesus Christ" (Gal 2:16) and that from this teaching comes the doctrinal statement of "justification by faith." Though the term may have a different nuance that belongs to God's judgment, here Jesus commands his disciples to "do righteousness" before God rather than before other human beings so that the Father can reward the doer of righteousness/justification.

Throughout the rest of Matthew 6, "doing righteousness" is clarified in terms of doing various spiritual practices that were typical for pious Jewish people: giving alms (6:2-4), praying (6:5-15; 7:7-11), fasting (6:16-18), refusing to trust in possessions on earth (6:19-24) but trusting in the Father's providence (6:25-34). However, as was Jesus' point with the various moral issues of Matthew 5, our Lord demands that his disciples go to the core issue underlying every spiritual practice: remain focused on the Lord God so as to come ever closer to him. He insists that his disciples avoid piety as a display for other people to see, which he identifies as "hypocrisy." The word "hypocrite" referred to an actor in a play: anyone who displays piety for mere human consumption is play-acting at discipleship instead of allowing God to relate to the person as a loving Father in ever-deeper ways.

CONSIDER

Jesus teaches a few other aspects of righteousness, particularly regarding the way his disciples are to treat other people. First, his disciples are instructed to avoid judging other people on the basis that it is difficult enough to understand oneself and one's own motivations: How can a mere human understand the motivations of other people?

 Stop here and read **Matthew 7:1-5** in your own Bible.

INVESTIGATE

GOD CAN READ THE "HEART AND MIND"

 Look up the following passages that indicate only God can read a person's "heart and mind."

PASSAGE	NOTES
1 Samuel 16:7	
1 Chronicles 28:9	
2 Chronicles 6:30	
Jeremiah 11:20	
Jeremiah 17:10	
Jeremiah 20:12	
Psalm 7:9	

Psalm 44:21	
Psalm 139:23	
Proverbs 17:3	
Romans 8:27	
Revelation 2:23	

In light of these verses, look up the following and note where Jesus knew what people were thinking in their minds without stating their thoughts.

PASSAGE	NOTES
Matthew 9:3	
Matthew 12:25	

Mark 2:6-8	
Luke 5:22	
Luke 6:8	
Luke 9:47	
John 2:24-25	
John 6:64	

STUDY

While human beings with limited ability to understand other people's hearts might not be able to judge the souls or inner motivations, they are still capable of making a judgment as to whether an external behavior is moral or not. On that basis, the disciples are instructed, "Do not give dogs what is holy; and do not throw your pearls before swine, lest they trample them under foot and turn to attack you" (Mt 7:6).

The "swine" and "dogs" are people who are incapable of grasping the Gospel, or at least its deeper parts. The Lord wants Christians to withhold the deeper teachings and mysteries of the faith until a person is capable of accepting it. Often this means building up a foundation for the faith until the person can comprehend various difficult elements. For instance, it is necessary for a Christian to believe in the Blessed Trinity — namely, that God is one God, but three co-equal divine Persons. However, it is not feasible to communicate this doctrine to someone who does not yet understand the difference between a nature and a Person, yet alone the divine nature and the divine Persons. A catechist does better to discern the capacity of the learner and lead the person by steps to a deeper understanding of the revelation of the three Persons in one God.

Discernment Required

Another area where Jesus permits and even requires the judgment of fellow human beings concerns the authenticity of false and true prophets. False prophets will destroy the Church the way a "ravenous wolf" would destroy a flock of sheep. Therefore, Christians must discern the true from the false prophet, both for their own sakes and for the sakes of other people who might easily become confused at their false teaching and/or bad morals.

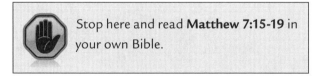

Stop here and read **Matthew 7:15-19** in your own Bible.

In the next session, we will examine various aspects of the judgment of the sheep and the goats in greater detail, but here it is sufficient to point out that when Jesus divides the nations into "sheep" on his right and "goats" on his left, he sets out the reasons on the basis of that he invites people into his kingdom.

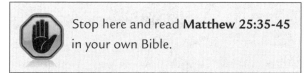

Stop here and read **Matthew 25:35-45** in your own Bible.

The criteria that Jesus uses in judging people are those that the Church now calls the *corporal works of mercy*. His criteria are a surprise to both the righteous and to the wicked, because neither group can ever recall having seen him in need. His response that whatever is done to the "least" solves the puzzle. Of course, he uses the very same criteria for the goats on his left who did not help the least of his brethren.

Jesus' teaching here highlights very clearly that performing these good works is necessary to our salvation; Christ will either accept people into heaven or send them to hell on the basis of performing these good works, so they are not nice options but are requirements for salvation.

St. John gives further insight into the importance of showing care for the poor and needy in 1 John 3:17-18: "But if any one has the world's goods and sees his brother in need, yet closes his heart against him, how does God's love abide in him? Little children, let us not love in word or speech but in deed and in truth."

Again, as St. James teaches, "a man is justified by works and not by faith alone" (Jas 2:24). Not only faith, but "in hope we are saved" (Rom 8:24), and love is also necessary for salvation. The works of mercy and the theological virtues — faith, hope, and love — are needed for salvation according to the word of God, and we do well to accept the "whole counsel of God" (Acts 20:27) in all of these matters of salvation.

CONSIDER

More from St. Paul

Of course, St. Paul is correctly well known for teaching that people are justified by their faith in Jesus Christ, as we have seen in the preceding lessons. However, like St. James, he does not in any way

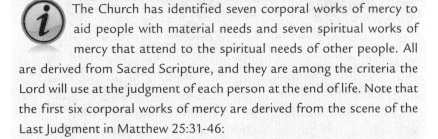 The Church has identified seven corporal works of mercy to aid people with material needs and seven spiritual works of mercy that attend to the spiritual needs of other people. All are derived from Sacred Scripture, and they are among the criteria the Lord will use at the judgment of each person at the end of life. Note that the first six corporal works of mercy are derived from the scene of the Last Judgment in Matthew 25:31-46:

1. Feed the hungry
2. Give drink to the thirsty
3. Clothe the naked
4. Welcome the stranger
5. Visit the sick
6. Visit the imprisoned
7. The last work of mercy — bury the dead — is derived from Tobit 1:16-22.

The spiritual works of mercy are also actions of love that are directed to other people's spiritual suffering:

1. Instruct the ignorant (Rom 15:14; Col 3:16; 2 Tim 3:14-17)
2. Counsel the doubtful (Mt 21:21-22; 28:17-20)
3. Admonish sinners (Ezek 33:7-9; Mt 18:15-17)
4. Forgive offenses (Mt 6:14-15; Mk 11:25)
5. Bear wrongs patiently (Mt 5:38-48)
6. Console the afflicted (1 Cor 14:3; 1 Thess 4:18)
7. Pray for the living, both friend (Rom 15:30; 1 Thess 5:25; 1 Tim 2:8) and foe (Mt 5:44), and for the dead (2 Mac 12:41-45)

All fourteen works of mercy are positive precepts that always bind us but are not always possible to make operative, such as when there is no occasion to do them or when a person lacks the material resources or ability to do them. Determining the actual obligation to perform a particular work depends on the degree of the need or distress, and the

continued on next page

neglect the necessity and importance of good works. Galatians is one of the two epistles most clearly identified with being justified by faith apart from the works of the Law, and yet St. Paul teaches that faith is necessarily linked with love: "For in Christ Jesus neither circumcision nor uncircumcision is of any avail, but faith working through love" (Gal 5:6). Faith works through love and in no way excludes actions of love but rather requires them. He told the Ephesians that doing good works is the reason we are created and therefore we live in accord with them: "For we are his workmanship, created in Christ Jesus for good works, which God prepared beforehand, that we should walk in them" (Eph 2:10). The goodness that people accomplish is linked to the fact that God created human beings, and therefore, it is linked to the purpose that is rooted in creation: to live according to "the image and likeness" of God. Since God creates things that are good, he therefore wants the human beings he created to accomplish good things in their lives in imitation of his own work.

An even more amazing statement about working out one's salvation appears in Philippians, the third epistle that has special treatment of being justified by faith.

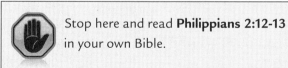

Stop here and read **Philippians 2:12-13** in your own Bible.

St. Paul lays out the mystery of God's grace operating within us as a free gift from him, and at the same time, our own choice to use the human gifts we possess in our human nature, including our free will and intellect, to work out our salvation. Remember that our human nature is itself a free gift from God: we do not choose our abilities, talents, gifts, and strengths before conception, since we did not exist until that point. Our whole existence is a gift from God, and yet God wants us to use the gifts he has given us in cooperation with his grace, which is a supernatural gift that strengthens a person's character interiorly to motivate the pursuit of holiness, goodness, truth, and beauty. This brings out the great mystery of the relationship between grace and free will.

THE WISDOM OF VATICAN II

From *Lumen Gentium* (n. 48):

Sitting at the right hand of the Father, he is continually active in the world that he might lead men to the Church and through it join them to himself and that he might make them partakers of his glorious life by nourishing them with his own Body and Blood. Therefore the promised restoration which we are awaiting has already begun in Christ, is carried forward in the mission of the Holy Spirit and through him continues in the Church in which we learn the meaning of our terrestrial life through our faith, while we perform with hope in the future the work committed to us in this world by the Father, and thus work out our salvation (cf. Phil 2:12).

STUDY

Two Poles of Salvation

Philippians 2:12-13 brings out two poles of the mystery of salvation. On one hand, St. Paul commands us to "work out" our own salvation, and on the other hand, he announces that "God is at work" in us "both to will and to work." This means that from our side of experience, we exert ourselves in "fear and trembling," not with some false confidence that I am absolutely certain that I am saved. It is certainly true that the truths of God are absolutely true and certain; however, "confidence" in humans is a subjective state and therefore not absolutely reliable. In contrast, a Catholic accepts the fallibility of a human act of certitude and therefore rejects the idea of possessing absolute certitude. Instead, based on a knowledge of human nature and its limited predictability, a Catholic ought to have "moral certitude," which is a proper confidence in a truth from God but a recognition that the human making the act of trust and confidence is changeable. This is not a lack of confidence in God and his truth but in human beings and their weak nature. Therefore, we are properly exhorted to have confidence without wavering.

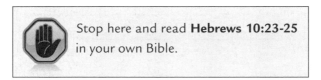

Stop here and read **Hebrews 10:23-25** in your own Bible.

We humans often need the exhortation to hold fast to our hope because life's difficulties and allurements might tempt us away from the hope that God gives us for our salvation toward immediate problems or pleasures. The antidote to wavering is the summons "to love and do good works," to meet with other Christians for regular worship, and to encourage one another. The alternative would be hypocrisy, as St. Paul described to his disciple, St. Titus, the first bishop of Crete: "They profess to know God, but they deny him by their deeds; they are detestable, disobedient, unfit for any good deed" (Titus 1:16). This means that the failure to do good deeds is a denial of God, which makes the hypocrites further incapable of doing good deeds — a downward spiral on the wide and easy path.

Salvation Earned by Works?

A very legitimate question posed by many non-Catholic Christians concerns whether Catholics believe that they are earning their salvation by their own efforts. The answer is a resounding no! Such a theology was held by a fourth-century British monk named Pelagius, but the Church rejected the idea that humans can save themselves by their own efforts and power without the interior grace of God. Scripture clearly teaches that doing good works is necessary for salvation, and yet it is impossible for humans to earn salvation by their own power and unaided efforts because they have offended the infinite God, and finite humans can never make up for the seriousness of their sins against God. How do these ideas fit together?

This mystery of the need of saving faith and of good works in order to be saved can be clarified by the scriptural teaching on grace. First, we read that God's free gift of grace saves us "through faith" and "for good works" together.

 Stop here and read **Ephesians 2:8-10** in your own Bible.

The consistent Catholic teaching is that saving faith is a gift of God's grace, along with saving hope and love, for which reason these three virtues are called "theological" — that is, possession of each depends on God's free and undeserved gift. Humans easily turn to self-congratulation and pride, so constant awareness of the fact that God redeemed us while we are still sinners will prevent us from boasting about our own goodness.

INVESTIGATE

"CREATED" FOR GOOD WORKS

 Take notes on the following, paying attention to how we were "created" for good works.

PASSAGE	NOTES
Matthew 16:27	
Romans 2:6	
2 Corinthians 5:10	
Revelation 2:23	

Revelation 20:12	
Revelation 22:10-12	

The omission of good works and the commission of evil "works of the flesh" threaten a person with exclusion from the kingdom of heaven for those who refuse to repent and have faith. Take notes on the following passages, noting the sins that are named.

PASSAGE	NOTES
1 Corinthians 6:9-10	
Galatians 5:19-21	
Ephesians 5:5	

Revelation 21:8	
Revelation 21:27	
Revelation 22:13-15	

God's Freely Given Grace

The issue is clearly serious indeed. How does one then live out the mystery of receiving undeserved free grace from God and doing the good works for which he created us and by which he will judge us?

What brings these elements of the mystery of salvation together is grace. Just as every person needs God's freely given grace in order to receive the gift of saving faith, so also does every person need God's freely given grace to become capable of doing the good works that he requires for our salvation. God's grace interiorly stirs humans to love him "with their whole hearts, minds and souls" and their neighbors as themselves. This grace of love motivates and empowers humans to overcome the disordered selfishness that results from original sin so that they can act selflessly in seeking to please God above all and to serve all of their brothers and sisters without regard to what they might get out of their self-giving. St. Paul therefore teaches us, "God's love has been poured into our hearts through the Holy Spirit which has been given to us" (Rom 5:5). This outpouring of the Holy Spirit is a gift that comes to us from the Father through Jesus. Through Jesus, the infinite Person of the Holy Spirit is "poured into" the depths of our hearts, and from deep within us he empowers us to love God and our neighbor with the infinite love that he is.

CONSIDER

At the Last Supper, Jesus used the image of a vine and its branches as another way to understand this mystery of our complete dependence on God as we bear fruit in good works.

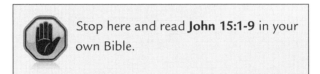

Stop here and read **John 15:1-9** in your own Bible.

Grapes do not grow on the main vine but on each individual branch; however, the branches cannot live or bear fruit unless they are united to the vine, from which they draw all of their nourishment. In this parable, Jesus wants us to see him as the vine who gives us our spiritual life and nourishment. Like a branch, we are completely incapable of staying alive and bearing fruit unless we are so united with him that we can say that we "abide" in him. The parable points to three options: if we do not bear fruit, we will be cut off and die; if we separate ourselves, we will die because no life comes into us; if we bear fruit, we will be pruned of the useless foliage so that we can bear more fruit. This, of course, refers to the ongoing spiritual and moral growth by which those elements of our personality that do not bear fruit for God are cut off, just as vinedressers prune or trim off the leaves and small branches that use up sap but produce no fruit. The Second Council of Orange, which was summoned in 529 to condemn the Pelagian heresy, uses this image of the vine and the branches in its understanding of the role of God's grace in enabling Christians to bear fruit in good works:

Canon 24. Concerning the branches of the vine. The branches on the vine do not give life to the vine, but receive life from it; thus the vine is related to its branches in such a way that it supplies them with what they need to live, and does not take this from them. Thus it is to the advantage of the disciples, not

GIFTED SO THAT WE CAN GIVE

An image I often use to understand this mystery comes from a personal experience when I was eight years old. Our family had just moved back to Chicago from Florida. I did not have a paper route or other job yet, but Dad wanted me to buy my mother a Christmas present. So he gave me a dollar and I went to a local mall — one of the first ever built in the country — and searched for a proper gift. Finally, I came to the "Community" store, an early discount store, where I found a small cross on a chain with a small purple stone at its center. When the cross was held up to the light, one could read the Our Father inside the stone. And it cost less than a dollar.

My dad made it possible for me to do something nice for my mother by giving me a dollar. I could have spent it on myself, but I knew that would be very wrong and would rightfully anger my dad. I bought the nicest thing I could find to make my mother happy. This was a good deed on my part, but it was at the same time totally a gift of my dad that made it possible to give a gift to Mom.

Similarly, God gives us his gifts so that we can give to others. In fact, everything in existence belongs to God who created it. He gives these things to us humans, and he wants us to please him by sharing these gifts with others, to make them happy. Even the love within us is his gift, but we cooperate with his gift by making a free choice to say yes to the task he gives us, or to refuse and act selfishly. This interplay of God's gracious gifts and our own free will is a great mystery, to be sure. However, the more deeply we give ourselves over to the life God gives us, and the more united we are to Christ the Vine, the more distinctive we become. We grow in love and become far better human beings precisely because we are letting his grace transform us into his image and likeness.

Christ, both to have Christ abiding in them and to abide in Christ. For if the vine is cut down another can shoot up from the live root; but one who is cut off from the vine cannot live without the root (Jn 15:5ff.).

The issue of doing works and becoming holy in order to be able to see God is closely connected to the issue of perseverance until the end of one's life. We turn to that subject in Session 6.

DISCUSS

1. What is the relationship of good works and faith to salvation? How would you explain this to a non-Catholic?
2. What would you say to someone who insisted upon the teaching of *sola Scriptura*? How does Catholic Tradition fit with Scripture?
3. Why do we need God's grace before we can do good works?

PRACTICE

This week, select one of the corporal or spiritual works of mercy and make a concerted effort to live it out in your daily life.

Session 6

PERSEVERANCE UNTO ETERNAL LIFE

 "You must be strong, dear brothers and sisters. You must be strong with the strength that comes from faith."

— POPE ST. JOHN PAUL II, Homily (June 10, 1979)

Some Christians teach that once a person repents and believes, that person is saved. A further doctrine that flows from "justification by faith alone" claims that once a person is saved, the person is always saved. This idea has its roots in the belief that justification by faith alone happens in a soul "by grace alone." Of course, the Catholic Church also believes that a person receives saving faith as a gift of God's freely bestowed and undeserved grace. However, as we have seen, Sacred Scripture and apostolic Tradition never teach that a person is justified by "faith alone." James 2:24 states just the opposite: "A man is justified by works and not by faith alone." Neither do we ever find the statement that justification comes by "grace alone": it is not written in Scripture.

CONSIDER

Doctrine of Total Depravity

The importance of recognizing this fact is not merely about proof-texts or verbally countering them. The real issue is that underlying the teaching of "justification by faith alone, by grace alone" are two false notions. The more basic of these two ideas is that original sin means that humans are not merely fallen but instead are totally depraved. From this flows the second idea: the human will is also so totally depraved that it cannot even say yes to God's grace, but God forces a person to accept grace or the person does not get forced to accept grace and is therefore condemned to hell. John Calvin, a prominent figure in the Protestant Reformation and founder of the Calvinist movement, wrote:

> Because of the bondage of sin by which the will is held bound, it cannot move toward good, much less apply itself thereto; for a movement of this sort is the beginning of conversion to God, which in Scripture is ascribed entirely to God's grace.... Therefore simply to will is of man; to will ill, of a corrupt nature; to will well, of grace. (*Institutes of the Christian Religion*, 2.3.5)

> We are all sinners by nature; therefore we are held under the yoke of sin.... "Confess that you have all these things from God: whatever good you have is from him; whatever evil, from yourself.... Nothing is ours but sin." (*Institutes of the Christian Religion*, 2.2.27)

Now Calvin's intention in this passage is not simply to rebuke men that they may repent, but rather to teach them that they have all been overwhelmed by an unavoidable calamity from which only God's mercy can deliver them, adding:

> Let this then be agreed: that men are as they are here described not merely by the defect of depraved custom, but also by depravity of nature. The reasoning of the apostle cannot otherwise stand: Except out of the Lord's mercy there is no salvation for man, for in himself he is lost and forsaken [Rom 3:23ff.] ... it is futile to seek anything good in our nature. (*Institutes of the Christian Religion*, 2.3.2)

Of course, from this doctrine flow a number of other key teachings. First, "unconditional predestination" starts with the idea that the human will is so depraved that it cannot choose anything that is good; and furthermore, since God makes a person accept grace or not, then it logically flows that God predestines some people to accept salvation and other people cannot. God therefore predestines some to heaven and some to hell; the human will is too weak to choose salvation and heaven, but it is depraved enough to deserve hell. This is sometimes called "double-predestination": God predestines who will go to heaven and who will go to damnation in hell.

Another idea that flows from the total-depravity doctrine is "limited atonement," by which Christ's saving death is limited only to save the elect. No one else gains any benefits from the atonement, nor can they, due to their depravity. A third idea is that God's grace is "irresistible," meaning that no human can resist it if God grants it. Finally, God will make the elect "persevere" in the faith, and so they are incapable of losing their salvation. This last idea flows from the notion that since God is the one who made them accept salvation, he would never allow them to fall away from it.

TULIP

"Total depravity," "unconditional predestination," "limited atonement," "irresistible grace," and "perseverance" form the acronym TULIP, which is a common way for folks to remember "Five-Point

THE WESTMINSTER CONFESSION

These doctrines come from John Calvin and his disciples and form the basis of the Westminster Confession that was drawn up in 1646 during the English Civil War between King Charles I and Parliament. This confession is used by various Presbyterian denominations, but it has also been modified many times since by Congregationalists (1658), Baptists (1689), and Presbyterians in the United States (1788 and 1903). Local congregations and the tens of thousands of new denominations that have started up over the years have widely varying acceptance of the Westminster Confession and its doctrines. Therefore, one ought not to assume that strict Calvinist doctrine is held by anyone unless one enters into a dialogue with a particular person to find out what he or she actually believes about total depravity, free will, predestination, and other related issues.

Calvinism." This is not so commonly held in modern times, leading one Five-Point Calvinist to tell me that he belongs to the 5 percent of the Baptist Church that is actually saved. Yet, even among those Protestants who have returned to the Catholic belief in free will, such as Billy Graham, who famously preached, "Make a decision for Christ today," they still maintain the Calvinist doctrine of "perseverance" in the form of "once saved, always saved." We will examine the Christian's need for perseverance until heaven, but from a more biblical perspective than TULIP permits.

CONSIDER

"Once Saved, Always Saved"?

The statement "once saved, always saved" is never found in the Bible, so it is necessarily a later doctrine and tradition invented by theologians. In fact, it is not taught among the Fathers of the Church nor in any of the councils. The goal of this doctrine, along with the other four points in the TULIP doctrine, was to emphasize the absolute majesty and greatness of God, the power of his grace and his divine will, the weakness of sinful human beings, and the absolute confidence people ought to have in God, his grace and salvation. Correctly, TULIP is meant to banish the idea that humans can earn salvation by their own power to do good works, a point of agreement with Catholic teaching. As we said earlier, good works are necessary along with faith to be justified, but God's grace makes it possible to do the good works, not the unaided human will. As the Second Council of Orange II put it in 529:

> **Canon 4.** If anyone maintains that God awaits our will to be cleansed from sin, but does not confess that even our will to be cleansed comes to us through the infusion and working of the Holy Spirit, he resists the Holy Spirit himself who says through Solomon, "The will is prepared by the Lord" (Prov 8:35, LXX), and the salutary word of the Apostle, "For God is at work in you, both to will and to work for his good pleasure" (Phil 2:13).

Canon 5. If anyone says that not only the increase of faith but also its beginning and the very desire for faith, by which we believe in Him who justifies the ungodly and comes to the regeneration of holy baptism — if anyone says that this belongs to us by nature and not by a gift of grace, that is, by the inspiration of the Holy Spirit amending our will and turning it from unbelief to faith and from godlessness to godliness, it is proof that he is opposed to the teaching of the Apostles, for blessed Paul says, "And I am sure that he who began a good work in you will bring it to completion at the day of Jesus Christ" (Phil 1:6). And again, "For by grace you have been saved through faith; and this is not your own doing, it is the gift of God" (Eph 2:8). For those who state that the faith by which we believe in God is natural make all who are separated from the Church of Christ by definition in some measure believers.

The point of contention between Catholics and other Christians is not whether God's grace is absolutely necessary, but rather the doctrines of "total depravity" and its consequences that water TULIP, with the complete incapacity of the human free will, versus the Catholic doctrine according to which original sin has weakened the human will so that it cannot make decisions to have faith, hope, or love without the grace of God, but it still has an important role of accepting or rejecting that grace.

The Council of Trent (1545-1563) affirmed the earlier council by saying the following:

Canon 1. If anyone says that man can be justified before God by his own works, whether done by his own natural powers or through the teaching of the law, without divine grace through Jesus Christ, let him be anathema.

Canon 2. If anyone says that divine grace through Christ Jesus is given for this only, that man may be able more easily to live justly and to merit eternal life, as if by free will without grace he is able to do both, though with hardship and difficulty, let him be anathema.

Canon 3. If anyone says that without the predisposing inspiration of the Holy Spirit and without His help, man can believe, hope, love or be repentant as he ought, so that the grace of justification may be bestowed upon him, let him be anathema.

Canon 4. If anyone says that man's free will moved and aroused by God, by assenting to God's call and action, in no way cooperates toward disposing and preparing itself to obtain the grace of justification, that it cannot refuse its assent if it wishes, but that, as something inanimate, it does nothing whatever and is merely passive, let him be anathema.

Canon 5. If anyone says that after the sin of Adam man's free will was lost and destroyed, or that it is a thing only in name, indeed a name without a reality, a fiction introduced into the Church by Satan, let him be anathema.

Because the Church does believe that human beings are fallen and therefore weak, she recognizes that every member of the Church must constantly seek the grace of God to enable the person to be remade in the image and likeness of God, and that God's graces come to every person who seeks them through prayer, the sacraments, sacramentals (holy objects) such as the Bible and other aids to faith, and the performance of the corporal and spiritual works of mercy. However, since the human will still retains its freedom of choice, each person must also choose to persevere in the faith, struggling against temptations that come from the devil, from the world, and from our fallen selves, and choosing to do that which is good for the sake of God and his people. For that reason, no Christian, apart from a special revelation from God, ought to assume that he or she is absolutely certain of salvation, as according to TULIP doctrines of perseverance. As the Council of Trent puts it:

Canon 16: If anyone says that he will for certain, with an absolute and infallible certainty, have that great gift of perseverance even to the end, unless he shall have learned this by a special revelation, let him be anathema.

A Christian can correctly hold to "moral certitude," that based on one's experience of life and the observable trajectory of one's behavior of faith, hope, and charity, one will be among the elect. One can correctly turn away from anxiety about hell to a confidence in God's love. Yet, it is necessary to persevere toward heaven with a recognition that God is absolutely trustworthy, but each of us must remain constantly vigilant and alert to the possibility that we might choose to act against his holy will. The Christian does not doubt God; it is on the self that one must keep an eye wide open.

STUDY

Faith in God and Human Weakness

We see this reality of tension existing over confident faith in God and the reality of human weakness in St. Paul.

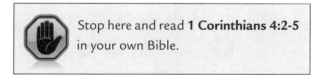

Stop here and read **1 Corinthians 4:2-5** in your own Bible.

No one can rightly accuse St. Paul of a lack of saving faith that justifies him, and yet he does not express absolute confidence that he is saved, either. He accepts no judgment from other people or even from himself, even though he is at that point unaware of any sin being held against him. He knows full well that the Lord is the judge and only he is able to know and understand the hidden depths of the heart. Any psychologist can describe how difficult it is for some clients to be honest with themselves regarding hidden motives and desires. In fact, a common reason for people to go to psychologists is to get help in understanding and accepting their hidden drives, desires, and feelings. Sigmund Freud pointed out a number of psychological defense mechanisms that prevent self-knowledge:

- *Rationalization* gives oneself logical excuses for one's problems.
- *Projection* attributes one's own bad behaviors, feelings, or thoughts onto other people.
- *Displacement* transfers one's negative feelings, especially anger, toward someone or something other than the real cause of the feeling because that feels safer.
- *Denial* rejects the painful or unpleasant real facts of life and its events so as to protect the person from difficult or painful emotions.
- *Repression* forces painful or frightening desires, emotions, and memories deep into the unconscious so that a person does not deal with them.
- *Regression* to an earlier state of development, often from childhood, is used to remove a person from present fears and anxieties.
- *Reaction formation* represses one particular fear by strengthening its opposite quality, as when very hostile people are sweet and nice to hide their anger or hostility.

These and other commonly observed psychological defenses prevent self-knowledge in fallen human beings, which is why it does not make sense to take salvation for granted.

The Possibility of Apostasy

The Letter to the Hebrews goes beyond St. Paul's recognition of the limits of his own self-knowledge and warns Christians of the possibility of deliberately turning away from salvation and the gift of the Holy Spirit to apostasy.

 Stop here and read **Hebrews 6:4-6** in your own Bible.

These verses recognize that Christians have partaken of the life of the Holy Spirit and of the goodness of God's word and the powers of grace of "the age to come," and yet they are able to commit the sin of apostasy, which Hebrews considers the same as crucifying Christ again and holding him up to contempt — a flat contradiction of the Calvinist TULIP doctrine of irresistible grace and perseverance without the possibility of ever falling away.

Stop here and read **Hebrews 10:26-27** in your own Bible.

This passage identifies deliberate sin that is committed "after receiving knowledge of the truth," which is another explicit denial of "once saved, always saved" theology. The reason the sin is deliberate is that these sinners still possess free will, and God's grace is not irresistible to a free person. They have the capacity to turn away from God's grace and then be judged with the prospect of damnation "and a fury of fire." The same teaching appears in 2 Peter.

Stop here and read **2 Peter 2:20-21** in your own Bible.

This speaks of people who have "escaped the defilements of the world" through Christ, but they become "entangled" in them again through sin and rejection of Christ. These verses show that Scripture teaches that God's grace is not irresistible; free will leaves room for the possibility that a person might "turn back from the holy commandment[s]" of God to serious sin.

This understanding of the ongoing possibility of sin also underlies some of St. Paul's warnings against committing sins that are so serious that they might keep a person out of the kingdom of God. At this point of our discussion, we do well to consider that St. Paul was addressing each of these warnings to Christians who had already repented, come to faith, and received the sacraments of Baptism and the Eucharist. In these passages, he warns them that any Christian who reverts back to evil deeds will forsake entrance into the kingdom of God and, thereby, end up in hell.

INVESTIGATE

DEADLY SINS

 Read the following passages and list the sins that are mentioned.

PASSAGE	NOTES
1 Corinthians 6:9-10	
Galatians 5:19-21	
Ephesians 5:5	

CONSIDER

At this point it is worth noting that those Christians who hold Five-Point Calvinist doctrine reject the idea that a Christian can commit mortal sin. With the denial of free will to do anything good, the "irresistible grace" and absolute perseverance make it impossible for a saved Christian to commit a mortal sin — that is, a sin that cuts off the life of grace in the soul. Of course, one problem with such a theology is that it contradicts Scripture again.

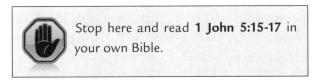

Stop here and read **1 John 5:15-17** in your own Bible.

While St. John does not use the word "venial," he distinguishes between mortal sins and sins that are not mortal. Later in Church history, the term "venial sin" was derived from the Latin word *venia* (meaning "indulgence, mercy, favor, pardon, and forgiveness") and therefore referring to a sin that could be forgiven simply by prayer. Of course, the term "mortal" (meaning "deadly") is used here as a metaphor for the death of the life of grace in the soul. The key to understanding mortal sin is that, as St. Thomas Aquinas puts it in his great work, *Summa Theologica*, it "is contrary to charity, which is the root of all the infused virtues." Since charity is "banished by one act of mortal sin," therefore "all the infused virtues are expelled" — that is, "faith and hope ... are no longer virtues." However, "venial sin is neither contrary to charity, nor banishes it," so "neither does it expel the other virtues."

In distinction to those who maintain the TULIP doctrines, the Catholic Church accepts the biblical teaching in 1 John 5:16-17 that all sin is wrongdoing, but some sins are mortal and can destroy the life of charity, faith, and hope inside a soul. Importantly, St. John wrote this toward the end of the first century (in the 90s) to the Christians of Ephesus and Asia Minor about their lives and not in reference to the sins of the pagans, just as St. Paul had warned the already converted Christians of Corinth, Galatia, and Ephesus in the 50s about the danger of losing their salvation because of the serious, or mortal, sins they had committed or might commit.

MORTAL VERSUS VENIAL SIN

Sin is a morally evil act, which can be chosen only by intelligent beings who know the difference between good and evil. What makes a sin evil is the lack of good — that is, a lack of conformity to right reason regarding the natural law and to the eternal law of God. Moral evil results whenever an intelligent creature who knows God and his law deliberately refuses to obey. This is a mortal sin when the matter of the sin is grave or serious (murder, adultery, inebriation, idolatry, and other serious sins), and the person knows it is gravely evil and willingly commits it. A sin is venial if the matter is not grave, or if the person does not know it is grave, or if the will is impaired in some way. This opens the way to a serious study of moral theology, which everyone can and ought to do, beginning with the *Catechism of the Catholic Church*.

CONSIDER

The Church and the Scriptures teach that we are summoned to be faithful to Christ, his teaching, and holiness until the day we die. At any point in life, we can turn away from God and become self-centered and commit sin, and we will be held accountable for such decisions throughout life. The Lord God instructed Ezekiel, the priest-turned-prophet, to warn the people of Israel about this, while they were in exile in Babylon.

> Stop here and read **Ezekiel 3:17-21** in your own Bible.

He repeats this message to Ezekiel, with an emphasis on the fact that the Lord will judge each individual as is appropriate to the person.

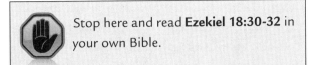

Stop here and read **Ezekiel 18:30-32** in your own Bible.

The underlying understanding of being human is that each person has intellect, which gives the power to know the available array of choices. That makes it possible for each person to have free will and therefore to obey God and choose to do what is good and self-giving, or to disobey God and choose what is evil and self-centered. One can make these choices all through life, since people are malleable like clay. However, death is the moment when the clay is fired and takes its permanent shape. That is why the decisions made at death are so determinative of eternal life, though it is important to know that the good habits and patterns that one develops throughout life make it easier to make the right decisions at death and more likely to do so.

This understanding of the way humans think and choose is the reason that Catholics do not maintain absolute certainty that once they have accepted salvation they will always remain faithful. Instead, based on the patterns and habits of faith, hope, and love that are developed throughout life, one can develop "moral certainty" — that is, the high likelihood of continuing a life of faith and virtue until death, without presumptuous certainty that salvation is already received.

STUDY

Given the assumptions we have just made about human nature and the ways that people relate to God, we turn now to some of Jesus' teachings on perseverance. Note that he never teaches that "once you are saved, you are always saved." Rather, he commands his disciples to persevere, implying that they have to exercise their free will and decide to remain faithful to him throughout their whole lives. We will examine four different types of occasion wherein Jesus instructs the disciples to persevere.

1. Perseverance in the Christian Mission to the World

The first occasion is when Jesus commissions the disciples for their first mission to the villages of Galilee, immediately after he identified the Twelve as his special envoys (see Mt 10). He sent them out with his own authority to extend his mission to the people of Israel.

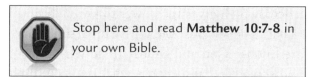

Stop here and read **Matthew 10:7-8** in your own Bible.

While the mission may have sounded exciting, Jesus did not want the disciples to be naive about the resistance that they would receive for accepting this mission. He let them know up front that they would be vulnerable to other people, including to those whom they loved. Note that Jesus warned the disciples about the risks of persecution because of their fidelity to the mission at various stages of his teaching.

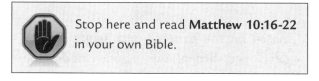

Stop here and read **Matthew 10:16-22** in your own Bible.

At the Last Supper, he taught them even more.

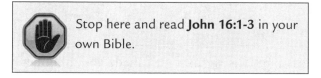

Stop here and read **John 16:1-3** in your own Bible.

The rejection of the disciples is ultimately not about the disciples' personality but results from a rejection of the Father and Jesus.

In Matthew 10:22, Jesus therefore points to the issue at stake in the disciples' perseverance in the mission until the end: "But he who endures to the end will be saved." The issue is not a mere career choice to preach, heal, and cast out demons, but one's salvation. In the light of the great importance of the outcome of their mission, the threats and power of those who oppose the Gospel are not a cause of anxiety because the salvation that Jesus offers them is worth the effort and the risk. Even if the enemies of the Gospel have the power to kill the body, they have no power over the soul of the faithful disciple. The only one to fear is the person "who can destroy both body and soul in hell" (Mt 10:28).

Again, even the disciple who has undertaken the mission in faith must remain alert to the need to remain faithful to Christ and persevere against the temptations that can destroy the soul by leading it into sin.

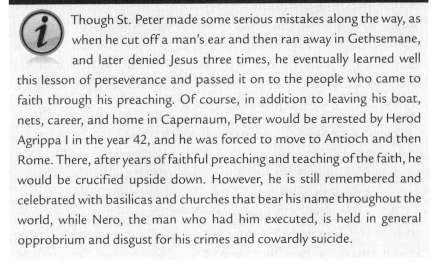

PETER, HEROD, AND NERO

Though St. Peter made some serious mistakes along the way, as when he cut off a man's ear and then ran away in Gethsemane, and later denied Jesus three times, he eventually learned well this lesson of perseverance and passed it on to the people who came to faith through his preaching. Of course, in addition to leaving his boat, nets, career, and home in Capernaum, Peter would be arrested by Herod Agrippa I in the year 42, and he was forced to move to Antioch and then Rome. There, after years of faithful preaching and teaching of the faith, he would be crucified upside down. However, he is still remembered and celebrated with basilicas and churches that bear his name throughout the world, while Nero, the man who had him executed, is held in general opprobrium and disgust for his crimes and cowardly suicide.

Of course, on the other side of Jesus' warnings that his disciples would be persecuted precisely because they were faithful, he also promises them "beatitudes." These are promises of becoming "blessed" or "happy" (two nuances of the Hebrew and Aramaic words underlying these beatitudes). The key to all of Jesus' beatitudes throughout the Gospels and New Testament is that he will reverse the expectations of the world and bestow a new type of blessedness upon his faithful disciples.

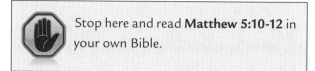

Stop here and read **Matthew 5:10-12** in your own Bible.

Naturally, the world would expect disciples to retreat from their mission of proclaiming moral righteousness or the message of Jesus and the kingdom of God in the face of threats or persecution. However, Jesus demolishes that false expectation by promising the persecuted disciples the kingdom of heaven and a great reward. This reward will outlast the kingdoms on earth and the various material rewards offered in this life, and the disciple is inspired by this promise to act far more nobly than those who pursue merely material rewards. Based on the promises that Jesus had made, St. James was able to inform his community of the same promises of becoming "blessed" with eternal life because of their love of God and steadfastness in the mission: "Blessed is the man who endures trial, for when he has stood the test he will receive the crown of life which God has promised to those who love him" (Jas 1:12).

2. Perseverance During the Agony in Gethsemane

A particular circumstance in which Jesus summoned his disciples to persevere in prayer took place after the Last Supper, when he went with them to Gethsemane, an olive press (*gath* means "press," and *shemen* means "oil") and garden. He already knew that Judas had betrayed him and that the traitor knew of his habit of praying in Gethsemane, so he fully expected to be arrested and taken to his passion and death from there. Leaving eight of the disciples in the small cave of the olive press, he took Peter, James, and John about "a stone's throw" away and made his first request to keep watch with him in prayer: "My soul is very sorrowful, even to death; remain here, and watch with me" (Mt 26:38).

Venerable Archbishop Fulton J. Sheen made that verse a jumping-off point for his call for people (especially priests) to make a Holy Hour of prayer before the Blessed Sacrament, especially for priests. He pointed out that Jesus had just ordained the apostles his priests and bishops at the Last Supper when he said, "Do this in remembrance of me" (Lk 22:19; 1 Cor 11:24-25), and the first thing he asked of them was to "watch with me" in prayer. The need for Christians to pray in the presence of Jesus Christ in the Blessed Sacrament whenever possible is to draw the strength they need for the other great difficulties and struggles of life, as modeled during the Agony in the Garden.

Jesus went a bit farther by himself to enter his prayerful communion with his Father, in a petition that the Father's will be accomplished on earth as in heaven, even though Jesus' human will resisted the suffering.

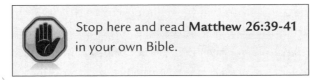

Stop here and read **Matthew 26:39-41** in your own Bible.

In this rebuke, we enter more deeply into the need for perseverance in prayer. Just as St. Paul had explained that his spirit had wanted to obey God's law but his flesh was weak (Rom 7:14-25), so also Jesus reminds his disciples that even when their spirit is willing to do what is good, their flesh is weak. For that reason, watchful prayer is able to strengthen weak disciples in times of stress and serious problems.

St. Mark and St. Luke report that Jesus spoke to the disciples in slightly different wording, also based on the last petition in the Lord's Prayer:

> **Mark 14:38**: "Watch and pray that you may not enter into temptation; the spirit indeed is willing, but the flesh is weak."

> **Luke 22:40-46**: And when he came to the place he said to them, "Pray that you may not enter into temptation." ... And when he rose from prayer, he came to the disciples and found them sleeping for sorrow, and he said to them, "Why do you sleep? Rise and pray that you may not enter into temptation."

"LEAD US NOT INTO TEMPTATION"

Many people wonder why the Our Father includes the petition "Lead us not into temptation," and Jesus' instruction on persevering in prayer in Gethsemane so that we might not "enter into temptation" highlights the issue. Of course, God does not tempt anyone: "Let no one say when he is tempted, 'I am tempted by God'; for God cannot be tempted with evil and he himself tempts no one" (Jas 1:13).

However, just as a general might lead his troops into a dangerous battle during a war, so might God lead his people into the danger of battle against evil and temptation. The general's purpose is to win the war, not to kill his soldiers. Similarly, the Holy Spirit led Jesus into the desert to be tempted so that he might overcome the devil, though with much prayer and fasting. This is the case for Christ's disciples as well. He calls us to persevere in prayer in order not to be led into temptation, but if we are so led, the prayer will strengthen us not to fall into it. This is a key lesson not only for the disciples but for us as well.

3. Perseverance in the End Times

The third circumstance in which Jesus admonishes his disciples to persevere is in the context of his teaching about the persecutions and other sufferings at the end of time. Though Jesus had spoken of the end of the world in a number of his parables and throughout his teaching, he began a longer discourse on the end times in response to the disciples' expression of wonder at the beauty of the Temple at sunset. However, having knowledge beyond the present moment, Jesus responded by announcing that the days were coming when there would not be left "a stone upon a stone," evoking a different kind of amazement and shock. In response, he launched into an explanation of two distinct events: the upcoming destruction of Jerusalem and its Temple, and the end of the world before the Last Judgment of all people. As he informed them of coming great catastrophes for Israel and for the world, which would be the "birth pangs" of the fullness of redemption, he emphasized their need to persevere through it all.

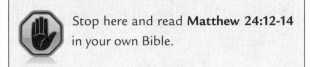

Stop here and read **Matthew 24:12-14** in your own Bible.

Jesus lets his disciples know that the people without faith will multiply their wickedness and their love will grow cold. As pointed out in earlier lessons, faith and love can be distinguished but ultimately not isolated from each other. On the other hand, his disciples will be saved if they "endure to the end." Christian perseverance in faith, hope, and love is not optional but necessary for salvation. Jesus never expects Christians to coast along on the fumes of past faith commitments or virtuous deeds; they are constantly and faithfully to follow him who is the "way" of life ("I am the way, and the truth, and the life" [Jn 14:6]). Until that point, Jesus gives us the task of preaching his Gospel of the kingdom of God to "all nations."

4. Perseverance in Suffering

Perseverance in faith, hope, and love until the end of life on earth is both for the normal, everyday times of Christian living and for the difficult times of suffering. Frequently, people lose heart during painful and difficult times of stress, but God does not treat those times as excuses for letting go of one's commitment. Instead, we read in James 1:2-4:

> Count it all joy, my brethren, when you meet various trials, for you know that the testing of your faith produces steadfastness. And let steadfastness have its full effect, that you may be perfect and complete, lacking in nothing.

Just as Jesus taught in the Sermon on the Mount, "Be perfect, as your heavenly Father is perfect" (Mt 5:48), St. James summons us to be "perfect and complete" even when that process of being perfected entails suffering during trials and testing.

By the end of the first century, there had already been a number of persecutions of the Church in Jerusalem, Rome, and a few other *i* "Eschatology" means the study of the end times. Jesus treats a variety of topics in his eschatological discourse in Matthew 24 and the other Synoptic Gospels — Mark 13, Luke 21 (John contains very little on this topic) — which we can mention in outline:

- **Matthew 24:15-22** describes the destruction of Jerusalem, using fairly standard images of war.

- **Matthew 24:23-28** warns against following false Christs, who will be dangerous imposters.

- **Matthew 24:29-31** foretells that cosmic changes will occur prior to Christ's judgment of the whole human race.

- **Matthew 24:32-41** admonishes the disciples to stay alert to the signs without being lulled by daily business.

Too often the focus is on making this type of study relevant by identifying contemporary events as the specific fulfillment of the prophecies, as if the writer knew more about it than the angels ("But of that day and hour no one knows, not even the angels of heaven, nor the Son, but the Father only" [Mt 24:36]). I like to point out that knowing the specifics of the end of the world is a management issue, and God is management. I'm only in sales. Our task is to preach the Gospel and be faithful to it, not figure out the dates of the end times, the identity of the Antichrist, and such. In fact, being ignorant of the specific date of our death is a mercy. Only one group knows that date — prisoners on death row — and such knowledge is a punishment.

Jesus does not expect his disciples to know the date of his Second Coming, and he even tells us that the angels do not know it. That is evidence that he does not expect us to try to figure it out. Rather, our readiness for his Second Coming is related more to the kind of wisdom we need to sustain us until he arrives.

places, and the antagonism toward Christianity was increasing in Asia Minor. However, with imprisonment and death as a real threat, the Lord insisted that Christians remain "faithful unto death." Their faithfulness will result in a crown of eternal life that the persecutors — despite all of their wealth, prestige, and power — will miss precisely because they are attacking Christ himself when they attack his followers. Finally, St. Paul encourages all Christians to put the reality of suffering into the proper perspective of a process that leads to God's glory.

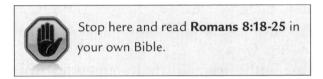

Stop here and read **Romans 8:18-25** in your own Bible.

Though suffering and persecution bring real suffering into the lives of Christians, we all do well to remember the promise of glory that will be "revealed to us." That glory far exceeds the suffering of individuals and of creation itself. The groaning is real; people do not enjoy the problems that flow from failure, economic stress, sickness, persecution, and death, whether of a loved one or of ourselves. Yet we put the suffering into perspective; it will not last anywhere close to the glory of heaven, and it will never be more powerful than the transformation that is in store for the adopted children of God, who will be empowered by the Holy Spirit to call God our "Abba, Father" for all eternity. That is the hope we await in patience until this life on earth is over. That is the hope that sustains Christians throughout the ages.

CONSIDER

Jesus' lessons on perseverance were neither lost nor forgotten by his apostles and disciples, who included this message in their various writings and linked it to salvation.

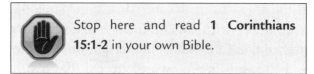

Stop here and read **1 Corinthians 15:1-2** in your own Bible.

St. Paul recognizes that the Corinthians have already "received" the Gospel "by which you are saved." However, they also are required to "hold it fast" and continue to live out every aspect of the Gospel throughout the entirety of their lives. If they do not "hold it fast," they turn their faith into a vain act. Clearly, this warning shows that Paul does not believe that once they are saved they are always saved. Rather, at every step of life the commitment to faith must be renewed and kept fresh.

The Letter to the Hebrews, which was written about a decade or so later, in the mid-60s for the Roman community, also exhorts Christians to persevere or suffer loss of salvation.

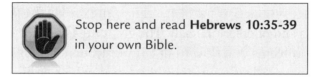

Stop here and read **Hebrews 10:35-39** in your own Bible.

Note that this section cites Habakkuk 2:3-4, as did St. Paul in Galatians 3:11-12 and Romans 1:17. However, along with highlighting the teaching that the "righteous one shall live by faith," as St. Paul did, Hebrews includes the rest of Habakkuk 2:4, which shows that the person who "shrinks back" from faith does not please the Lord. On that basis, Hebrews exhorts us not to be among those "who shrink back," because the issue at stake is whether we keep our souls or not. The person who "shrinks back" is in danger of losing his or her soul. Therefore, "confidence," "endurance," and perseverance enable us to "do the will of God and receive what is promised."

STUDY

Jesus concludes his discourse on the destruction of Jerusalem and on the end of the world with four parables about the Lord's judgment of various types of people. We do well to consider all four of them in some detail so as to gain deeper insight into both the need for perseverance and the various aspects of the judgment that Jesus Christ will mete out to each and every person on earth.

Faithful Versus Wicked Servant

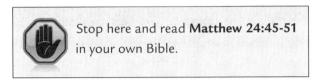

Stop here and read **Matthew 24:45-51** in your own Bible.

The parable of the faithful and wicked servants is primarily about the leaders of the Church community that Jesus has begun by his ministry. Throughout his public ministry, the Lord has called leaders and attracted them by great love. However, he has never refrained from criticizing and rebuking the leaders for their wrongdoing (recall how Jesus rebuked Peter as "Satan" for trying to silence his message about his upcoming suffering and death). Jesus opens the first parable with a rhetorical question about the identity of the faithful and wise servant and answers it with a beatitude and a statement of reward.

The promise of beatitude belongs to the "faithful" servant who is "wise" (in Greek, *phronimos*), which refers to the type of practical wisdom that knows how to get things accomplished. This is different from the more common term for wise, *sophos*, which has a more reflective quality to it. The servant's tasks include leadership over the household and serving the other people at the right time. Jesus explained this kind of leadership to his disciples earlier when they became envious of placement and position in Matthew's Gospel:

> But Jesus called them to him and said, "You know that the rulers of the Gentiles lord it over them, and their great men exercise authority over them. It shall not be so among you; but whoever would be great among you must be your servant, and whoever would be first among you must be your slave; even as the Son of man came not to be served but to serve, and to give his life as a ransom for many." (Mt 20:25-28)

However, the servant who leads faithfully and prudently will be rewarded with beatitude from his master, who is Christ himself, and will share in even greater leadership.

INVESTIGATE

 This promise is similar to that which Jesus made to the Twelve about sitting on twelve thrones to judge the twelve tribes of Israel as a direct share in his leadership. Read the following and make notes.

PASSAGE	NOTES
Matthew 19:28	
Luke 22:28-30	
1 Corinthians 6:2-3	
2 Timothy 2:11-13	
Revelation 2:26-28	

Jesus also describes attitudes and actions of a wicked servant, adding the threat of a bad end in Matthew 24:48-50:

> But if that wicked servant says to himself, "My master is delayed," and begins to beat his fellow servants, and eats and drinks with the drunken, the master of that servant will come on a day when he does not expect him and at an hour he does not know, and will punish him, and put him with the hypocrites; there men will weep and gnash their teeth.

The wicked servant excuses his behavior by denying the near approach of the master. Assuming that his behavior will have no consequences, he then acts with overbearing power against his fellow servants and uses his master's property as if it were his own. Of course, Jesus makes it clear that the master will return and will summon every servant to account. However, the time of that return is unknown and unexpected to the servants.

"CUT IN TWO PIECES"

For the wicked, the punishment is immediate and eternal: the first verb "punish" in Greek means "cut in two pieces." This is an idea that goes back to the Middle Bronze Age, when punishment for breaking a covenantal commitment was to be cut in two pieces from top to bottom (see Gen 15:9-21, when Abram splits some animals in two pieces before the smoking brazier passes between the pieces). The second part of the punishment is to be placed with the hypocrites who weep and gnash their teeth in eternal regret for their hypocritical "play-acting" at being religious. Such "wailing and gnashing of teeth" is a frequent description of eternal torment in Matthew's Gospel.

Wise and Foolish Virgins

Stop here and read **Matthew 25:1-13** in your own Bible.

The second parable uses the image of ten women awaiting the arrival of a bridegroom for the wedding celebration in order to teach the importance of watchful preparedness. The setting for the parable is the wedding feast.

A simple statement that five virgins were foolish and five were wise is followed by an explanation of why they were so different. What made five of them "wise" was their cleverness in practical knowledge and foresight regarding their possible need for oil for their lamps in case the bridegroom was delayed. The Lord commends their prudence because he wants us to be clever, just as he had commended to his disciples before their first mission: "Behold, I send you out as sheep in the midst of wolves; so be wise as serpents and innocent as doves" (Mt 10:16).

In this parable, the oil simply represents a practical necessity, but it points to everything we may need in order to be prepared for the coming of Christ, the Bridegroom of the Church.

On the other hand, the key problem of the foolish virgins is that they thought they knew how short would be the time of the bridegroom's delay. They are like those Christians who have identified specific dates and years for the Second Coming of Christ. As a result of one preacher's certain conviction that he knew that Christ was coming in May 2011, a few of his followers even sold their homes and used up their savings. His followers were homeless and without money when the prediction failed, and he became despondent. While I still feel grief and sorrow for him, I cannot help but see that his action parallels the foolish virgins, who did not bring enough oil for the bridegroom's long delay.

The greater crisis comes with the arrival of the bridegroom at midnight. It is worth noting that in the Middle East, weddings commonly are delayed because the groom's and the bride's parents continue to negotiate the dowry or other concerns. This detail fits the culture. However, the groom does arrive at midnight and the ten virgins are summoned to meet him in order to lead him in a procession to the wedding feast. The foolish virgins propose taking some oil from the wise, but once again the wise have enough foresight to know that neither group would have enough oil to keep their lamps burning. Therefore, as the wise virgins enter the feast, the foolish go looking for oil.

Sadly, upon their return they see that the door to the wedding feast is closed, excluding them from the banquet, so they enter a dialogue with the bridegroom. Note that the five foolish virgins also address the bridegroom as "Lord, Lord" and hear him reply, "I never knew you." Foolishness may be a key element in being the kind of person Jesus does not know, and it is certainly the ultimate folly not to let Jesus know oneself. The parable of the ten virgins concludes with an admonition, "Watch therefore, for you know neither the day nor the hour" (Mt 25:13).

Christ does not want disciples to use his delay of the Second Coming to ever become an excuse for their lack of preparation, prudence, or of being known by him. No one ought to begin the Christian life with a kind of enthusiasm that is lived in a lack of preparedness. As the *Didache* (16:1), an early Christian treatise, says in referring to this passage about watchfulness: "Be watchful for your life. Let not your lamps be quenched, and let not your loins be ungirded, but be ready, for you do not know the hour in which your Lord comes."

INVESTIGATE

THE WEDDING FEAST OF HEAVEN

Keeping in mind all of these passages of nuptial imagery for the relationship between the Lord and Israel in the Old Testament, and between Jesus Christ and the Church in the New Testament, it is logical to understand heaven as a wedding feast. In the following passages, take note of the nuptial imagery.

PASSAGE	NOTES
Matthew 9:15	
Matthew 22:2	

Mark 2:19-20	
Luke 5:34-35	
John 3:29	
2 Corinthians 11:2	
Ephesians 5:25-27	
Revelation 19:7	
Revelation 21:2	
Revelation 21:9-11	

The Polish weddings I attended in my youth are joyful memories, as are the Lebanese weddings I have helped celebrate over the past years of being bi-ritual in the Maronite Rite. They are not meant to let the families be conspicuous in spending their money so as to show off to friends and neighbors a willingness to waste a lot of money. Rather, the families seek to share their goods in an effort to extend a joyful welcome to the friends and relatives of the bride and groom as an important step in helping strangers build the bonds of family that will strengthen as the newly married couple have children and celebrate baptisms, birthdays, First Holy Communions, the weddings of their children, and milestone anniversaries. Weddings look forward to a lifetime of future celebrations of new life, and the role of weddings to introduce various in-laws is a way to start bonds of love that will deepen as all family members together come to love the new family.

The Servants and Their Talents

> Stop here and read **Matthew 25:14-30** in your own Bible.

The third parable about the three servants receiving talents is not so much focused on the Lord's unexpected arrival as it is on the activity of the faithful disciples during the master's absence. The parable opens with a man entrusting his three servants with different numbers of talents as he begins a journey. A key component is the Lord's absence and the activity of his servants. (A talent was a measure of money tallied in different ways. It equaled 6,000 denarii, with each denarius being a day's minimum wage. A talent was also about 65 pounds of gold or silver. By either standard, each talent was a very large amount of money.) The center of attention of the entrustment of the talents is the ability of each servant. Individuals can handle various kinds of responsibility, some more and others less. Jesus recognizes the variation in human ability and adapts to each person's qualifications, without dismissing the less-qualified person as useless. He simply does not give as much responsibility to the less-qualified people.

Next, the parable describes the actions of the three servants with their talents, wherein each of the first two servants trade with the money and double it, but the third hides it. The master then returns to settle accounts with the three servants and judges each one, as a clear representation of the return of Christ as a judgment scene. Two of these servants are good and faithful because of their industrious effort to increase the master's money. Even though the talents still belong to the master, they have labored to increase his property. Their reward is twofold: first, they have an increase in responsibility because they demonstrated that they are capable of this; second, they enter into the joy of their master. This joy may derive from the increased responsibility and the potential for deeper human ability. However, this joy may also be a new level of fellowship with the master. This share in the master's joy as an increase of responsibility relates to the promise that Christ made to the Twelve that they would sit on twelve thrones judging the twelve tribes of Israel.

However, when the master settles accounts with the wicked and lazy servant, things do not go well for him. The servant approaches the master with the original talent and an excuse for not prospering. Instead of mentioning the amount he had received, as the other servants had done, this servant begins to excuse himself by describing the hardness of his master. He is judging the master who has arrived to actually judge him. For that reason, the master rebukes the servant.

The servant is called "wicked and slothful" or lazy. His fault lies in the lack of industrious activity and initiative out of fear of failure rather than the lack of increase for its own sake. As such, he epitomizes the servant who is not awake or watchful. The second stage of punishment occurs when the worthless servant is sent outside in great personal torment to weep and gnash his teeth. In the last verse of this passage, the "wailing and gnashing of teeth" is a phrase which the Lord uses frequently to describe the torture of being excluded from the kingdom of heaven that he had come to announce and to which he has invited all people.

"The Least of These My Brethren"

Stop here and read **Matthew 25:31-46** in your own Bible.

In this fourth parable, Jesus teaches that he will return to judge all people at the end of the world, using the works of mercy for his criteria, as we examined in the preceding session. Here we will center on Jesus in the judgment rather than on the criteria.

Matthew opens the scene by describing the coming of the Son of Man on his glorious throne, accompanied by his angels. Three other times in Matthew, Jesus describes himself as the "Son of Man" who has his own angels and the authority to judge humans:

> "For the Son of man is to come with his angels in the glory of his Father, and then he will repay every man for what he has done." (Mt 16:27)

> Jesus said to them, "Truly, I say to you, in the new world, when the Son of man shall sit on his glorious throne, you who have followed me will also sit on twelve thrones, judging the twelve tribes of Israel." (Mt 19:28)

> "But I tell you, hereafter you will see the Son of man seated at the right hand of Power, and coming on the clouds of heaven." (Mt 26:64)

We do well to remember that this description is based on a prophecy from Daniel.

Stop here and read **Daniel 7:13-14** in your own Bible.

That prophecy helps explain the importance of the next part of Jesus' teaching when the nations will be gathered for judgment by the Son of Man. This scene portrays Jesus as a shepherd, just as he had done earlier and would do again at the Last Supper. Here he is a shepherd with the supreme authority to separate the good from the evil, as a shepherd separates sheep from goats.

An important indicator that Jesus has the authority to judge all of the nations is his promise to send the disciples to preach to the nations. If he has the authority to commission the disciples to preach to all nations, then he has the authority to judge them all. This authority became part of the content of the disciples' preaching, as we see in Acts 17:30-31:

> The times of ignorance God overlooked, but now he commands all men everywhere to repent, because he has fixed a day on which he will judge the world in righteousness by a man whom he has appointed, and of this he has given assurance to all men by raising him from the dead."

CONSIDER

The Bottom Line

Jesus taught that the central point and goal of doing righteousness is for a person to go to heaven and to avoid condemnation and suffering in hell. This is clear in the parables of the kingdom of heaven in Matthew 13:44-46, where Jesus compares the kingdom to a treasure hidden in a field or a pearl of great price, for which nothing else is more valuable. It is like a dragnet "at the close of the age," when the angels will "separate the evil from the righteous" and either "throw them into the furnace of fire" or keep them for God (Mt 13:49-50). Obviously, nothing else in human life is as important as the decision to pursue the kingdom of God and avoid being thrown "into the furnace of fire."

Similarly, in the Sermon on the Mount, Jesus poses a warning to his followers about the decision to enter heaven or go to hell by saying that the way to hell is wide and easy but the way to eternal life in the kingdom of heaven is narrow and hard: "Enter by the narrow gate;

for the gate is wide and the way is easy, that leads to destruction, and those who enter by it are many. For the gate is narrow and the way is hard, that leads to life, and those who find it are few" (Mt 7:13-14).

This warning is to motivate Christians to be sober and alert about the issues at stake in making decisions about virtue and righteousness or vice and sin. The stakes are high, and many assumptions in the culture are not the same as those of Jesus Christ.

The basic assumption underlying this Bible study is that salvation is not jumping through hoops to cover every step as if it were a mathematical or scientific formula. Rather, salvation is a rich mystery that every human sinner is called by God to live and of which every Christian is a steward. Jesus Christ leads any and every sinner to ever greater depths of salvation through the whole of one's life. Certainly, some key points of conversion occur when a person makes a decision to repent — that is, turn away from the painful and destructive path that leads to perdition. Deciding against self-centered choices that disregard God, other people, and the beauty of creation presents new directions toward God and toward love of our neighbors for their own sakes rather than for the things they might be able to do for us. These are conversion points that often stand out as determinative points of faith — we accept that God exists, that Jesus can forgive our sins and give new purpose to life, that life is better when we love others rather than wait for them to serve us.

However, after repenting — that is, of turning from the wrong paths of life — comes the living out of those decisions on a daily basis. We learn to integrate the meaning of faith in God and his truths, hope in the future that God sets before us, and love God with our whole heart, mind, and soul and love our neighbor as our self. These pathways can also be sources of various kinds of struggles to integrate new truths from God about him, ourselves, and our neighbors, as they form new assumptions about the ways we think, decide, and act. Yet no Christian can afford to forget that these experiences are as integral to one's salvation as are the key points of conversion.

Perhaps a simple image is to see the moments when we make the determinative decisions to convert to faith, hope, and love as mountaintop experiences. These are high points of our lives that can even overwhelm a person emotionally, intellectually, and spiritually. These mountaintop experiences give us new perspectives on the whole meaning of life, and they present wide vistas from which we can see the potential catastrophes of our sinful past and the glories of the future that God offers his saints.

The everyday living of the Christian life is more like walking down the mountain to the valleys. The vistas are not so dramatic, but in fact there are far more things growing in the valleys than on the mountaintops, as any mountain climber can explain. In fact, mountain climbers survive because they take food from the valleys with them to the top! Furthermore, the plants and animals growing in the valleys each possess their own kind of beauty and usefulness. Perhaps they seem humbler than the mountaintop views, but they are more edible and sustaining than a vista.

Both aspects of the spiritual pilgrimage through life toward heaven complement each other and are good for us. We humbly accept these and many other gifts that God might give us with gratitude and appreciation. We learn surprising new lessons about God, ourselves, and life. Even as we await "our blessed hope, the appearing of the glory of our great God and Savior Jesus Christ" (Titus 2:13), we take life in this world seriously, as the Church has always done. For that reason, Christians invented notions such as the hospital, orphanage, mental asylum, university, and school systems. Christians believe that "when Christ who is our life appears, then you also will appear with him in glory" (Col 3:4). Yet throughout this life on earth they are inspired to seek and express fantastic beauty in architecture and the arts that is directed to the worship and honor of God — basilicas, cathedrals, sculptures, paintings, music, and literature by Michelangelo, Dante, Vivaldi, and many others.

Throughout the centuries, Christians have been willing to "endure everything for the sake of the elect, that they also may obtain salvation in Christ Jesus with its eternal glory" (2 Tim 2:10). Like St. Paul, "for the sake of Christ," they have been "content with weaknesses, insults, hardships, persecutions, and calamities" knowing that "when I am weak, then I am strong" (2 Cor 12:10). The 75 million Christian martyrs — including the 40 million of the twentieth century — show that their faith and love of Christ Jesus is more important than life itself because "there will be richly provided for you an entrance into the eternal kingdom of our Lord and Savior Jesus Christ" (2 Pet 1:11). These martyrs and those who survive them heed the words of St. James: "Be patient, therefore, brethren, until the coming of the Lord. Behold, the farmer waits for the precious fruit of the earth, being patient over it until it receives the early and the late rain" (Jas 5:7).

Whether facing martyrdom or living a more ordinary life of raising a family in the love of God, every Christian should remember this: "Do you not know that in a race all the runners compete, but only one receives the prize? So run that you may obtain it" (1 Cor 9:24). We all run to obtain the "prize" of eternal life and love. Following Christ's narrow path is filled with adventures, growth, and wisdom.

Come.

Follow him.

DISCUSS

1. How can you have confident faith in your salvation and yet not fall into the error of "once saved, always saved"?
2. What are the four circumstances in which Jesus admonishes the disciples to "persevere"? How can you apply these circumstances to your life?
3. What are your "talents"? Are you investing them wisely in your life?

PRACTICE

Choose one of the parables discussed in this session and meditate on it. Imagine yourself in the scene. What do you see? What do you smell? What can you touch? Create as vivid a picture as you can, and then ask yourself, "What does Jesus want me to learn from this parable?" Sit quietly and let an answer fill your heart.

LAST WORDS

Before we conclude these lessons, we do well to pick up the exclamation of praise and wonder at the tremendous salvation that Jesus Christ has effected for sinners that St. Paul wrote to the Romans and make it our own act of praise and worship:

> For God has consigned all men to disobedience, that he may have mercy upon all. O the depth of the riches and wisdom and knowledge of God! How unsearchable are his judgments and how inscrutable his ways! "For who has known the mind of the Lord, or who has been his counselor?" "Or who has given a gift to him that he might be repaid?" For from him and through him and to him are all things. To him be glory for ever. Amen. (Rom 11:32-35)